MASTERING PIZZA

Mastering Pizza

**Unlocking the Secrets to World-Class Recipes.
Pizza, Calzone And Focaccia at Home!**

Written By **MARK SELL**

© COPYRIGHT 2020 BY MARK SELL - ALL RIGHTS RESERVED.

This document is geared towards providing exact and reliable information concerning the topic and issue covered. The publication is sold with the idea that the publisher is not required to render accounting, officially permitted, or otherwise, qualified services. If advice is necessary, legal or professional, a practised individual in the profession should be ordered. From a Declaration of Principles which was accepted and approved equally by a Committee of the American Bar Association and a Committee of Publishers and Associations. In no way is it legal to reproduce, duplicate, or transmit any part of this document in either electronic means or printed format. Recording of this publication is strictly prohibited, and any storage of this document is not allowed unless with written permission from the publisher. All rights reserved. The information provided herein is stated to be truthful and consistent, in that any liability, in terms of inattention or otherwise, by any usage or abuse of any policies, processes, or directions contained within is the sole and utter responsibility of the recipient reader. Under no circumstances will any legal obligation or blame be held against the publisher for any reparation, damages, or monetary loss due to the information herein, either directly or indirectly. Respective authors own all copyrights not held by the publisher. The information herein is offered for informational purposes solely and is universal as so. The presentation of the data is without a contract or any guarantee assurance. The trademarks that are used are without any consent, and the publication of the logo is without permission or backing by the trademark owner. All trademarks and brands within this book are for clarifying purposes only and are owned by the owners themselves, not affiliated with this document.

CONTENTS

Mastering Pizza
Introduction
Art of Italian Pizza
Mediterranean Pesto Pizza
Boboli Pizza Crust Recipe
Boboli Type Pizza Crust Recipe
Model Pizza Crust Recipe
Cornmeal Pizza Crust Recipe
Crucial Dish Pizza Crust Recipe
Essential Pizza Dough Recipe
Heart-Shaped Pizza Recipe
Herb Pizza Dough Recipe
Pizza Dough Recipe
New York Style Pizza Dough Recipe
New York-Style Pizza Crust Recipe
Pizza Crust Recipe
Pizza Dough (Bread Machine) Recipe
Pizza Dough and Sauce Recipe
Polenta Pizza Crust Recipe
Pourable Pizza Crust Recipe
Delicate Pizza Dough Recipe
Entire Wheat Pizza Crust Recipe
Fundamental Pizza Sauce Recipe
Firehouse Pizza Sauce Recipe
Pizza Sauce II Recipe
South Beach Diet Simple Pizza Sauce Recipe
A-1-DERFUL Mini Pizzas Recipe
Alsatian Bacon and Fresh Cheese Tart Recipe
Artichoke Turkey Pizza Recipe
Bacon Cheeseburger Upside-Down Pizza Yield
Bacon Onion and Tomato Pizza Recipe
Bacon Spinach Pizza Recipe
Arranged Pizza Sandwich Recipe
Cheeseburger Tortilla Pizza Recipe

Breakfast Pizza Recipe
Broccoli Turkey Pizza Recipe
Air pocket Pizza Recipe
Butternut Squash, Bacon, And Rosemary Pizza Recipe
Camper's Pizza Recipe
Canadian Bacon Pizza Recipe
Bacon Pizza Recipe
Pancetta Pizza Recipe
Cheddar Steak Pizza Recipe
Mushy Jalapeno and Egg Pizza Recipe
Ciro's Pizza Recipe
Club Pizza Recipe
Corncake Pizza Wheels Recipe
Corn Tortilla Pizzas Recipe
Crazy Crust Pizza Recipe
Crazy Crust Pizza II Recipe
Straightforward Bake Oven Deep Dish Pizza Recipe
Fig and Prosciutto Pizza Recipe:
New Tomato and Basil Pizza Recipe
Gluten-Free Rice Crust Pizza Recipe
Goat Cheese and Walnut Pizza Recipe
Chicago-Style Deep-Dish Pizza Recipe
Brilliant Gate Pizza Recipe
Hawthorne Lane's Pepperoni Pizza Recipe
Natively constructed Pizza Recipe
Custom made Pizza Recipe
Frank Pizza Recipe
Singular Pesto Pizzas with Mushrooms and Olives Recipe
Child-Sized Pizzas Recipe
Child-Sized Southwest Pizza Recipe
Leek Tomato Goat Cheese Pizza Recipe
Minimal English Muffin Pizzas Recipe
Make-Ahead French Bread Pizza Recipe
Mexican Salmon Pizza Recipe
Microwave Mini Pizzas Recipe
Mushroom Turkey and Swiss Cheese Pizza Recipe
Parsley Pesto and Feta Phyllo Pizza Recipe
Peking Duck Pizza Recipe

Philly Cheese Steak Crescent Pizza Recipe:
Pita Pesto Pizzas Recipe
Pizza Arizona Recipe
Pizza for Easy bake Oven Recipe:
Pizza Pesto Verde Recipe
Pizza Rustic Recipe
Pizza Santa Fe Style Recipe
Pizza with Pork and Peppers Recipe
Polenta Pizzeria Recipe
Spring Up Pizza Casserole Recipe
Potato Pizza Bake Recipe
Prosciutto Tomato Pizza Recipe
Outside layer
Pumpkin Pizzas Recipe:
Reuben Pizza Recipe
Firm Sweet Onion Pizza Recipe
Exciting Salmon Pizza Recipe
Messy Joe Pizza Recipe
Smoked Salmon and Fennel Potato Pizza Recipe
Smoky Salmon Pizza Recipe
Southwest Beef and Chile Pizza Recipe
Spam Pineapple Pizza Recipe
Stuffed Crust Pepperoni Pizza Recipe
Exceptional Pizza Recipe
Thai Pizza II Recipe
French Bread Pizza Recipe
Tri-State Pizza Recipe
Truffle Pizza Recipe
Turkey Club Pizza Recipe
Topsy turvy Pizza Recipe
White Onion Pizza Recipe
White Spinach Pizza Recipe
Onion Pizza Recipe
Grill Chicken Pizza Recipe
Profound Dish Mexican Pizza Recipe
Mayonnaise Burrito Pizzas Recipe
A spot outside layer on a massive heating sheet
Flame-broiled Chicken Pizza Recipe

Barbecue Chicken and Bacon Pizza Recipe
Boursin Chicken Pizza Recipe
Wild bull Chicken Wing Pizza Recipe
For the Chicken
California Pizza Kitchen's Thai Chicken Pizza Recipe
Burrito Mexicali Pizza Recipe
Colorado Calzoni

MASTERING PIZZA

Introduction:

An astonishing player finished with tomato sauce and a holder heap of cheddar; pizza is a finished dish for any exacting eater in your home. For adolescents, pizza is reliably seen as one of their supported sustenance's while for grown-ups, it is seen as one of the most advantageous dinners around. From the capacity to fuse your supported fixings, there is every so often a sort of pizza that isn't respected by in any event one individual.

If you love pizza and have, for a long time, been shivering to make pizza inside the solace of your own home, by then, you have vehemently gone to the ideal spot. Inside this through and through pizza cookbook, you will get capacity with each bit of pizza making, from making the player feasibly, to raising the mix, setting up the sauce to organizing the pizza with the ideal improvements. I accept that you will end up being a pizza-making capable shockingly quick.

At present, we quit relaxing around and get to cooking!

ART OF ITALIAN PIZZA:

The historical backdrop of pizza starts in days of yore when different antiquated societies delivered fundamental flatbreads with a few fixings.

A forerunner of pizza was likely the focaccia, a level bread referred to the Romans as pains focaccias, to which fixings were then added. Modern pizza advanced from comparative flatbread dishes in Naples, Italy, in the eighteenth or mid-nineteenth century.

The word pizza was filed for the first time in 997 AD. in Gaeta and gradually spread from central to southern Italy. The pizza was eaten mainly in Italy and by people in exile from that point. Soldiers positioned in Italy came to appreciate pizza alongside other Italian nourishments.

MEDITERRANEAN PESTO PIZZA:

On the off chance that you love the flavour of Mediterranean cooking, at that point, this is a pizza dish I realize you will become hopelessly enamoured with. With pita flatbreads for the most delicious outcomes.

Makes: 2 servings. Total Prep Time: **15 minutes**

Ingredients:

1) 2 Tbsp. of pesto
2) 6-inch Greek pita flatbreads
3) 1/2 cup of feta cheese
4) 2 tomatoes, slashed
5) 8 Kalamata olives, boneless

Method:

1) Heat the oven to s50 degrees.

2) Spread the prepared pesto on every pita flatbread.
3) Finish off with the feta cheese, slashed tomatoes, and Kalamata olives.
4) Transfer the focaccia to the baking tray.
5) Place into the oven to heat for 8 to 10 minutes.
6) Remove and serve right away.

BOBOLI PIZZA CRUST RECIPE:

Ingredients:

1) A pack of dry yeast

2) 1/4 cup of water

3) 1/4 cups of hot water

4) Six tablespoons of olive oil, + extra for the pan

5) 6 cups of flour

6) A teaspoon of salt

Direction:

Separate yeast in warm water (1050F is unfathomable). Let it sit for two minutes. Consolidate the remainder of the ingredients and blend well. Turn out onto board and control for ten minutes. Spot back in bowl ensured about with a light towel and let rise 30 to 40 minutes.

Segment mix into three sections and spot in 3 olive-oiled pie skillets. Dimple player with fingers. Spot on top the going with blend: Coarse ocean (or Kosher) salt, crisp ground pepper, cut rosemary, and thyme. If herbs are dried, hold the water for 10 minutes and from there on pat dry on paper towels.

Let rise 50 to an hour. Warmth at 350 F for 25 minutes. May plunge in olive oil.

BOBOLI TYPE PIZZA CRUST RECIPE:

Ingredients:

1) 1 cup of water
2) 3 cups all around helpful flour
3) 1 teaspoon salt
4) 2 tablespoons olive oil
5) 1 tablespoon sugar
6) 2 teaspoons Red Star dynamic dry yeast
7) 1 teaspoon minced garlic
8) 2 teaspoons parmesan cheddar
9) Parmesan cheddar to sprinkle

Method:

Fuse all ingredients (close to) second parmesan cheddar to bread maker all together recorded by your maker. It is a quick plan to put the garlic down inside the flour, so it doesn't slow the yeast. Set bread maker on mix setting. Right, when complete, structure two covers on pizza holder, sprinkle with parmesan cheddar, spread, and let rise once more. Prepare 5-10 minutes at around 450 F until light darker.

Cool. Wrap emphatically in foil and freeze until you get the pizza to engage. Incomprehensible to have around for direct a minute earlier dinner. Phenomenal course for children to make pizza too.

MODEL PIZZA CRUST RECIPE:

Ingredients:

1) One pack dry yeast
2) 2 1/2 cups flour
3) One teaspoon salt
4) 1 cup of warm water
5) One tablespoon cooking oil

Method:

In a gigantic blending bowl, cement the yeast, 1 cup of flour, and the salt. Blend. Next, fuse the water and oil. Beat on low speed for 30 seconds. Scratch the sides of the bowl and keep beating on speedy for 3 minutes. By hand, mix in enough flour to make the mix stable. Back rub until smooth, which can take as long as 10 minutes. Spot in an especially lobed bowl and turn the player until it is delicately lobed.

Spread and let move for around 1/2 hours or until the hitter has copied. Hack the hitter down the inside. On a floured surface, overlay the parts into 12-inch float and around 1/8 inch thick. Brush the surfaces of the player with olive oil and join your supported fixings. Cook at 425* for 25 minutes.

CORNMEAL PIZZA CRUST RECIPE:

Ingredients:

1) 1 cup of warm water
2) 1/4 teaspoon salt - discretionary
3) 2 1/2 cups flour
4) 1 cup cornmeal
5) 1 tablespoon cornmeal
6) 2 tablespoons sugar
7) 2 teaspoons dry yeast

Method:

Measure watchfully, setting with or without ingredients from 1 tablespoon cornmeal in bread machine dish all together obliged by proprietor's manual. Program central mix cycle setting; press start. Expel player from bread machine skillet; let rest 2 to 3 minutes.

Pat and cautiously stretch mix into a 14-to 15-inch circle. Sprinkle a 14-inch pizza skillet with non-stick cooking shower; sprinkle with staying one tablespoon cornmeal. Press player into the skillet. Follow fixing and warming bearing for specific plans. One 14-INCH outside layer makes eight servings

CRUCIAL DISH PIZZA CRUST RECIPE:

Ingredients:

1) 3 cups flour
2) 1/8 cup olive oil
3) 2 eggs
4) 2 tablespoons thyme
5) 1 cup of warm water
6) 1 pack yeast
7) 2 teaspoons sugar

Method:

Put aside to demand for 10 minutes. In a considerable bowl channel together flour and salt and sprinkle in thyme. Blend eggs into yeast blend. Void fluid into dry ingredients and blend until a dubious persisting player structure. Void mix to a meticulously floured surface and control 5 minutes, until the player, isn't, eventually gainful.

A spot in a particularly oiled bowl, going to cover all sides, spread and award to move until reached out in mass 2 - 3 hours. Punch mix down and place into an all-around oiled 12" pizza dish. Utilizing your hands, move mix around the base of the dish, and 2/3 the course up the sides. Put in an ensured spot and let rise 10 minutes. Brush covering carefully with olive oil and harden fixings.

ESSENTIAL PIZZA DOUGH RECIPE:

Ingredients:

1) 3 1/2 cups unbleached, all-around favorable flour
2) 2 packs dry bewildering yeast

Method:

In a blending bowl fitted with a player get, place flour, yeast, salt, and sugar. While the blender is running, a tiny bit at a time merges water and control low speed until the player is firm and smooth, around 10 minutes. Turn the machine off. Pour oil down inside a bowl. Turn on low again for 15 seconds to cover inside the bowl and all surfaces of the mix in with the oil. Spread bowl with stick wrap. Let hitter move in a warm spot until recreated in mass, around 2 hours. Preheat stove to 500 degrees F. On the off chance that is utilizing a pizza stone, place the stone in the stove on-base rack, preheat barbecue 1 hour ahead. Punch mix down, cut down the middle. Spot half of the player on liberally floured work surface. By hand, structure mix plainly into a ball and stretch into a circle. Utilizing floured moving pin, overlay hitter into large buoy until flimsy. Put forward an undertaking not to push if your circle isn't uncommon, and on the off chance that you get an opening fundamentally squash the edges back together. To shield hitter from holding energetic to counter, turn over the mix and sprinkle with flour. Also, flour the edge and moving pin separating. Sprinkle pizza strip or treat sheet liberally with cornmeal. Move mix to pizza strip or treat sheet with no lip. Join fixings. Slide player onto the pizza stone or spot treat sheet with pizza on-base rack. Prepare 10 to 12 minutes or until confounding. Turn out an extra hitter and top with required fixings or freeze in cooler packs.

HEART-SHAPED PIZZA RECIPE:

Ingredients:

1) 1 cup of water
2) Two tablespoons milk
3) Two teaspoons sugar
4) 1 1/4 teaspoon salt
5) One tablespoon olive oil
6) 2 cups of durum wheat semolina flour
7) 2 cups unbleached bread flour
8) 1 1/4 teaspoon yeast

Method:

Spot water, milk, sugar, salt, shortening, and olive oil in a bowl of sustenance processor and heartbeat to disengage sugar and salt. Join yeast, semolina or corn dinner, bread flour, and all-around consistent flour. Framework until a delicate ball structure. Expel from machine and award to rest, ensured about with a towel, around 45 minutes.

Or then again obviously to make by hand: Use just conventionally critical flour. Spot water, milk, sugar, salt, shortening, and olive oil in a bowl and separate sugar and salt. Mix in the yeast, semolina or corn supper, generally significant flour, and back rub to plot a delicate, yet not unusually steady hitter (8-10 minutes). Award to rest assured about with a towel around 45 minutes.

Void hitter cautiously before utilizing and permit it to rest 15 minutes more before utilizing it in a condition. You may refrigerate hitter in an oiled plastic sack for as long as two days. Shape mixes into a heart. Top with your supported sauce and fixings. Warmth in a hot stove 425 - 450°F. for 15 - 20 minutes.

HERB PIZZA DOUGH RECIPE:

Ingredients:

1) One pack Active Dry Yeast
2) One teaspoon Sugar
3) 7/8 cup Warm Water - 110 degrees
4) 1/4 cup Italian Seasoning
5) 2 1/4 cups Flour
6) One tablespoon Flour
7) 1/2 teaspoon salt
8) One tablespoon Garlic Olive Oil
9) Oil and Cornmeal for Pan

Method:

Join the yeast, sugar, and warm water. Let remain until frothy, around 10 minutes. In the work bowl of a sustenance processor fitted with the steel forefront, cut the herbs. Perspective killer machine. Add flour and salt.

Turn the machine on and off different events. While the machine is running, join yeast. Framework until the player diagrams a ball along the edge of the bowl. Union garlic olive oil and structure for 30 to 40 seconds more.

Move mix to a bowl that has been oiled with olive oil. Turn the player until the whole surface has been guaranteed about with the oil. Spread bowl with a supple towel and permit to move in a warm draft-free spot for 1 hour or until broadened.

Turn out on a meticulously floured surface, and if the mix is an over the top proportion of versatile, have a go at heaving it from hand to hand to level it out. Carefully oil the pizza skillet with a little oil and sprinkle with cornmeal. See the player on the pizza skillet and trim the edges. Warmth for 10 minutes @ 425 degrees. Expel from broiler, delicately brush the outside layer with genuinely more oil. Top varying. Makes enough mix for one 12" covering.

PIZZA DOUGH RECIPE:

Ingredients:

1) 1 1/2 teaspoon bread machine yeast
2) 3 cups flour
3) 3/4 cup milk
4) Two tablespoons olive oil
5) 1/2 cup lukewarm water
6) 1 1/2 teaspoon salt
7) pinch sugar

Method:

Spot all ingredients except water in a nourishment processor. Heartbeat to blend well. At that point, turn the machine on and shower the water in until it shapes a ball. Release the ball around a couple of times in the machine to work it a piece. Expel mixture onto a floured surface and manipulate well for a couple of moments until flexible.

Spot in a lobed bowl and let ascend until multiplied. Expel from the bowl and punch down. Cut into two pieces and turn out into four medium-size outside layers, enough to take care of 4 individuals. Turn broiler on and preheat at 400°F for 30 minutes, if utilizing pizza stone. If no stone, preheat broiler to 400°F for 10-15 minutes. Spot pizza outside layer on the rear of a heating sheet that has been secured with a sprinkling of cornmeal. A spot in stove and heat for 8 minutes. Evacuate and spread with garnishes. Spot back in stove and heat for eight additional minutes until the covering is brilliant and cheddar is bubbly.

NEW YORK STYLE PIZZA DOUGH RECIPE:

Ingredients:

1) 1 1/2 cup warm water
2) 2 1/2 teaspoons granulated sugar
3) 2 1/2 teaspoons salt
4) 1 tablespoon olive oil
5) 4 1/2 cups flour
6) 1/2 teaspoon dry yeast
7) 1/2 cup cornmeal
8) sauce, cheddar

Method:

In a considerable bowl, break up sugar and salt in water. Add oil and flour to the bowl and mix with a solid spoon for one moment. Press into a circle. Sprinkle yeast uniformly over mixture and work for 12 minutes. Gap mixture into divides: 4 equivalent bits for calzones, three equivalent parts for 8" pizzas, two equivalent bits for 12" pizzas. Spot batter balls in a bowl spread with saran wrap, and permit to ascend for 1/2 hours in a warm area. Spot a batter ball on a daintily floured surface and sprinkle a light covering of flour on top. Working from the edges to the inside, press batter into a circle. Preheat a pizza stone in a 500-degree stove for 60 minutes. Spot the smoothed mixture onto the cornmeal. Spread sauce over outside and top with cheddar and wanted garnishes. Tenderly shake the slicing board from side to side, guaranteeing it isn't adhering to the board. For a calzone, overlay the hull over into equal parts.

Legitimately onto the stone in the stove. Prepare in a 500-degree stove for 20-25 minutes until the outside layer is brilliant.

NEW YORK-STYLE PIZZA CRUST RECIPE:

Ingredients:

1) 2/3 cup warm water
2) 1/2 teaspoon salt
3) 2 1/4 cups generally useful flour
4) One teaspoon sugar
5) Two teaspoons dry yeast
6) One tablespoon cornmeal - discretionary

Method:

Measure cautiously, putting all ingredients except cornmeal in bread machine container all together indicated by proprietor's manual. Program batter cycle setting; press start. Expel batter from bread machine container; let rest 2 to 3 minutes.

Pat and tenderly stretch batter from edges until the mixture appears not to extend any longer. Let rest 2 to 3 minutes more. Keep tapping and extending until the mixture is 12 to 14 creeps in the distance across. Shower 12-to 14-inch pizza dish with cooking splash; sprinkle with cornmeal, whenever wanted. Press mixture into the dish. Preheat stove to 450°F. Follow garnish and preparing headings for singular plans, heating pizza on the base rack of the barbecue.

PIZZA CRUST RECIPE:

Ingredients:

1) 0.47 L warm water (110F - 115F)
2) 59 milliliters olive oil
3) Two bundles yeast
4) 1 2/5 L flour
5) 9 9/10 milliliters of salt yellow cornmeal

Method:

Evidence yeast with support in warm water. Blend yeast, water, and olive oil mix in flour 1 cup at once. Turn out onto the floured surface, ply until smooth, 5 to 7 moments, including flour as necessary. The batter will be delicate. A spot in an oiled bowl, going to cover all sides. Punch down and let rest 15 mins. Partition down the middle a, press out into two 12-inch round pizza dish or 10x15x1 skillet or 1 of each. Sprinkled with yellow cornmeal (prevents outside layer from staying).

PIZZA DOUGH (BREAD MACHINE) RECIPE:

Ingredients:

1) 1 cup water "PLUS"
2) Two tablespoons water
3) Two tablespoons oil
4) 3 cups bread flour
5) One teaspoon sugar
6) One teaspoon salt
7) 2 1/2 teaspoons dry yeast

Method:

Spot ingredients in the dish all together recorded or as coordinated per machine directions. Select the white mixture cycle. Makes two 12-inch standard outside layers or one 16-inch dish hull. Top with necessary fixings and prepare at 400°F for 18-20 minutes or until the covering is light darker.

PIZZA DOUGH AND SAUCE RECIPE:

Ingredients:

1) 3/4 tablespoon yeast
2) 1 1/2 cup water
3) 1 1/2 teaspoon salt
4) Three tablespoons oil
5) 4 cups flour
6) 6 ounces thick tomato sauce
7) 1/2 cup wine or water
8) One teaspoon oregano
9) One teaspoon salt
10) One tablespoon sugar
11) One tablespoon vegetable oil or olive oil
12) 1 1/2 tablespoon parmesan cheddar

Method:

Break down yeast in water (You can include a touch of sugar). Mix in salt, oil, and half of the flour. Continuously include remaining flour, blending great. Work 8-10 minutes or until smooth and flexible. Spot in a lobed bowl and let ascend until twofold (1/2 60 minutes). Punch down and let rise again until twofold.

Punch down and isolate. Work out on pizza dish. Top with pizza sauce and fixings. Heat at 400 for 20-25 minutes. Pizza Sauce: Mix all ingredients, mixing great (You can likewise include a couple of sprinkles of garlic powder if you need). Top with meats, cheddar, and different fixings.

POLENTA PIZZA CRUST RECIPE:

Ingredients:

1) One tablespoon Active dry yeast
2) One tablespoon Barley malt extricate
3) 1 cup of warm water
4) 3/4 cup semolina
5) 1 cup unbleached generally useful flour
6) 3/4 cup polenta/corn dinner
7) One teaspoon salt
8) Three tablespoons additional virgin olive oil

Method:

In a considerable bowl or electric blender, break up the yeast and grain malt in warm water. Include the semolina, flour, polenta, salt, and olive oil. Join well. Massage the batter until it is sparkly and smooth, including flour varying. Spot the batter in a softly oiled bowl, spread with cling wrap, and let ascend until multiplied, around 2 hours.

At the point when the batter has risen, punch down and turn out to a large circle and move to a preparing sheet or pizza skillet. Top with any favored fixing and prepare in a preheated 425F grill for 20 - 25 minutes. This is acceptably topped with broiled veggies.

POURABLE PIZZA CRUST RECIPE:

Ingredients:

1) Three tablespoons Instant High-Active dry yeast
2) Warm water (110 degrees F) (just enough to break up the dynamic yeast)
3) 7 pounds or bread flour
4) One bundle (1 lb. 2 1/2 oz.) Instant nonfat dry milk
5) 8 3/4 ounces Sugar
6) 1 1/4 teaspoon salt
7) 1/8 cup Olive oil
8) Cornmeal

Method:

Break up dry yeast in warm water. =20 Let stand 5 minutes. Spot flour, milk, sugar, and salt in the blender bowl. Utilizing a whip, mix on low speed for 8 minutes. Include disintegrated yeast and oil. Mix on medium speed for 10 minutes. The player will be uneven. Oil three sheet container (18" X26" X1").

Sprinkle each dish with 1 oz (around 3 Tbsp) cornmeal. Pour or spread 3 lb 6 oz (1/2 quart) player into each container. Let represent 25 minutes. Prepare until the outside layer is set: Conventional Oven: 475 degrees F, 10 minutes. Convection Oven: 425 degrees F, 7 minutes. Top each prebaked outside with wanted garnish. Prepare until warmed through, and cheddar is dissolved: Conventional Oven: 475 degrees F, 10-15 minutes. Convection Oven: 425 degrees F, 5 minutes.

DELICATE PIZZA DOUGH RECIPE:

Ingredients:

1) 3 cups bread flour
2) 7/8 cup warm water
3) One tablespoon vegetable shortening (Crisco)
4) One teaspoon dynamic dry yeast
5) One teaspoon salt
6) 1/2 teaspoon sugar

Method:

In a blender with a mix get, combine water, fat, yeast and sugar. Blend until the yeast has completely dissolved. Add flour and salt. Blend until mixed, then continue checking for 10 minutes. The mix will be free from the start and will eventually structure a thick dough. There should be no flour in the bowl. The kneader will be, to a certain extent, dry and dense. Take the dough and wrap it in plastic wrap. Place it in the refrigerator for 24 hours before using it. Put forth an attempt not to dodge this development!

Preheat your broiler to 500 F around one hour before you hope to warm the pizza. Turn the mix out onto a large surface and development with flour. Utilizing a fantastic moving pin, turn the hitter out flimsy to plot a 24-inch or more prominent circle. On the occasion that you're utilizing a shaper pizza dish (prescribed), dust the skillet tenderly with flour, place the hitter in the compartment, and dock. Utilize the moving pin to trim off the abundance mix hanging over the sides of the dish. Cook the pizza genuinely on a pizza stone (not utilizing a holder), by then recognize the mix on a cleaned pizza-strip, dock, and overlay the edge more than 1-INCH straightforwardly around and pound it up to layout a raised lip or edge.

Next, precook the outside layer for 4 minutes before including any sauce or fixings. Expel the outside layer from the flame broil and pop any large air pockets that may have shaped.

Fuse your sauce, wrecked mozzarella cheddar, and your supported fixings. Keep warming, turning the skillet for the most part through with the target that it cooks unbiasedly, until the covering is adequately caramelized and fresh, around 10 to 15 minutes. Expel the pizza from the flame broil and slide the pizza out of the cooking holder onto a large wire cooling rack or cutting board. Award to cool for 5 minutes before moving to a serving dish. This development permits the outside layer to remain fresh while it cools; in any case, they got steam will release up the edge. Right when cold, utilize a pizza shaper to cut the pie into pieces and appreciate it!

ENTIRE WHEAT PIZZA CRUST RECIPE:

Ingredients:

1) 1 1/4 cup warm water
2) 1/4 teaspoon salt - discretionary
3) 2 tablespoons nectar or sugar
4) 2 cups of white flour
5) 1 cup entire wheat flour
6) 2 teaspoons dynamic dry yeast
7) 1 tablespoon cornmeal

Method:

Measure carefully, setting all ingredients aside from cornmeal in bread machine skillet all together directed by proprietor's manual. Program mix cycle setting; press start. Expel mix from bread machine holder; let rest 2 to 3 minutes. Pat and gently stretch mix into a 14-to 15-INCH circle. Sprinkle 14-inch pizza compartment with non-stick cooking shower; sprinkle with cornmeal, at whatever point required. Press hitter into the dish. Follow adorn and preparing headings for specific plans. One thick 14-INCH outside layer is eight servings

In a large pot, delicately sauté the onion in the oil until direct. Add the tomatoes and bring them to the air pocket. When stewing, fuse the tomato puree, the vinegar, and sugar. Stew for an entire hour, utilizing a wooden spoon to disconnect any tomato pieces. On the off chance that the sauce, regardless of everything, has bits of tomato, experience a strainer before constraining and dealing with in the cooler for to around fourteen days. Spread pathetically on pizza, use over pasta with a ground, robust, hard cheddar, or use as a base for continuously complex meat sauces for pasta.

FUNDAMENTAL PIZZA SAUCE RECIPE:

Ingredients:

1) 35 ounces canned entire tomatoes
2) One teaspoon basil
3) One clove garlic, stripped and squashed
4) Two tablespoons tomato stick
5) salt and pepper - to taste

Method:

Pour the substance of the tomato can into a 2-quart, extensive non-aluminum holder and coarsely pound the tomatoes with a fork. Consolidate the herbs, garlic, tomato glue, salt, and pepper. Bring to an air pocket over medium warmth, stirring to blend the seasonings.

Exactly when the sauce starts to bubble, turn the sparkle to low and keep up the sauce at a delicate stew. Cook, revealed, stirring from time to time, for at any rate 15 minutes and an imperative of 60 minutes.

FIREHOUSE PIZZA SAUCE RECIPE:

Ingredients:

1) 1 (6 ounces) tomato
2) 3/4 cup warm water (110 degrees F/45 degrees C)
3) Three tablespoons ground Parmesan cheddar
4) One teaspoon minced garlic
5) One tablespoon Honey
6) One teaspoon anchovy (discretionary)
7) 3/4 teaspoon onion powder
8) 1/4 teaspoon dried oregano
9) 1/4 teaspoon dried marjoram
10) 1/4 teaspoon dried basil
11) 1/4 teaspoon ground dull pepper
12) 1/8 teaspoon cayenne pepper
13) 1/8 teaspoon dried red pepper chips

Method:

In a little bowl, harden tomato stick, water, Parmesan cheddar, garlic, Splenda, anchovy stick, onion powder, oregano, marjoram, basil, ground diminish pepper, cayenne pepper, red pepper pieces, and salt; unite, disconnecting any heaps of cheddar. Spread over pizza players and plan pizza varying.

Mince onion and garlic. Sauté in olive oil until onion is transparent and delicate. Add the rest of the ingredients to skillet and stew for 15-20 minutes. Makes enough sauce for two pizzas. Additionally, makes a beguiling sauce for breadsticks and calzones.

Slash onion and garlic, microwave for five minutes (discard this progression if you don't have a microwave; it isn't basic; however, it makes the sauce faster to cook). Move to the pan, include tomato puree and mix. Include tinned tomatoes. Season, bring to bubble, and stew for around 15-20 minutes until it has diminished to a jammy consistency. For flavoring, I utilize salt, crisply processed dark pepper, Worcestershire sauce, and a herb, new basil if I have it, or dried Italian flavoring.

PIZZA SAUCE II RECIPE:

Ingredients:

1) Three tablespoons olive oil
2) Three cloves garlic, minced
3) 28 ounces entire cooked tomatoes
4) One tablespoon dried oregano
5) One teaspoon dried basil
6) Salt and pepper to taste

Method:

Warm olive oil with garlic on medium warmth. Mix and cook for 2 to 3 minutes. Include depleted and seeded tomatoes alongside salt, pepper, oregano, and basil at that point mix and cook for 15-20 minutes until sufficiently thick to spread over pizza mixture.

Consolidate tomato glue, garlic, parsley pieces, onion, oregano, basil, and water in a 2-quart pot. Cook over medium-high warmth until blend bubbles. Decrease warmth to low and stew 10 minutes. Cool marginally and spread on pizza outside layer; top as wanted and heat.

SOUTH BEACH DIET SIMPLE PIZZA SAUCE RECIPE:

Ingredients:

1) One tablespoon tomato glue
2) 1 cup tomato puree
3) 1/8 teaspoon squashed red pepper pieces
4) Two teaspoons dried oregano
5) Two teaspoons dried basil
6) Two teaspoons dried thyme

Directions:

Consolidate all in little pot and cook over low warmth for 15 minutes, or until sauce thickens.

Put starting five ingredients in a container. A tiny bit at a timed race in milk until no bunches remain. Warmth and blend until foaming and thickened. Blend in margarine until disintegrated. Spread on pizza outside layer; top with most adored embellishments. Unbelievable with grilled chicken strips on top!

A-1-DERFUL Mini Pizzas Recipe:

Ingredients:

1) 3/4-pound ground burger 1/4 cup minced onion
2) One can (6 oz. size) tomato stick three tablespoons A.1. Steak sauce
3) One teaspoon Italian herb seasonings 6 English bread rolls, split and toasted 2 cups cut mozzarella cheddar ground parmesan cheddar
4) 1/4 cup cut green onion Directions:

In tranquilize. Skillet, cook and break down meat until not, now pink; channel. Incorporate the onion and cook until sensitive. Mix in tomato stick, steak sauce, and Italian herb seasoning; cook until mix stews.

Spread bread leaves behind the meat mix. Top with cheeses and green onion. Spot on getting ready sheets. Singe 2 to 4 minutes or until cheddar is mollified.

ALSATIAN BACON AND FRESH CHEESE TART RECIPE:

Ingredients:

1) dry yeast
2) 1/2 cup warm water
3) 4 cups of bread flour, with 1/2 cup of cold water
4) A spoonful of extra virgin olive oil, per bowl
5) 1/4-pound piece bacon cubed one tablespoon olive oil
6) 1/2 cup of thinly sliced yellow onions
7) Three tablespoons of yellow cornmeal, a large egg
8) 3/4 cup whole milk ricotta cheddar three tablespoons plain yogurt

Method:

The flammkuchen, or "blasting tart," is the Alsatian adjustment of pizza. All through the area, you'll find commonplace bistros that make a distinguishing strength of the dish. The floppy tarts are brought out from the wood-expending grill on a wooden strip, slid clearly onto the table, and ate up while they are about too hot to manage.

In a gigantic mixing bowl, join yeast and the warm water Let speak to 5 minutes Stir with a fork to blend Add 1/2 cup of the bread flour and blend well Cover and let stand 45 minutes Add the infection water and salt Begin including bread flour 1 cup immediately, blending incredible after each choice When player ends up being too firm to even think about evening consider mixing, move to a delicately floured surface and handle until smooth and reflexive (7 to 10 minutes) Place in a gently oiled bowl and go to cover blend with oil Cover and let climb until increased in mass, around 1 3/4 hours In a medium skillet over moderate warmth, render bacon in olive oil until bacon fat is melted and bacon is caramelized Transfer bacon to a plate with opened spoon and add onion to skillet Sauté until insignificantly mellowed (around 5 minutes) Cool to room temperature Preheat grill to 425 F Dust a pizza stone or significant warming sheet with cornmeal Whisk together Fromage Blanc, egg, and the 1 Tbsp flour Punch down blend and crease into as tremendous a circle or square shape as will fit on the warming sheet Transfer to orchestrated getting ready sheet Spread with Fromage Blanc mix to inside 3/4 inch of edge Top with onions and rendered bacon and sprinkle with ground cheddar Brush edge of blend with the 2 Tbsp water Bake until splendid dim hued (15 to 20 minutes)

ARTICHOKE TURKEY PIZZA RECIPE:

Ingredients:

1) 1 arranged thin Italian pizza outside layer (12-inch size)
2) 1 1/2 cup crushed Mozzarella cheddar
3) One can (14.5-ounce size) diced tomatoes with basil, garlic, and oregano, drained
4) 1 cup severed cooked turkey
5) One can (14-ounce size) artichoke hearts, drained, coarsely cut
6) One can (2.25-ounce size) cut olives
7) 1/2 cup of grated Parmesan cheddar

Method:

Preheat oven to 450 degrees F. Spot outside layer on ungreased warming sheet. Sprinkle with mozzarella cheddar. Top with tomatoes, turkey, artichokes, olives, and Parmesan cheddar. Warmth 10 minutes, or until cheddar is condensed. In a medium significant skillet cook prosciutto and onion in oil over moderate warmth, mixing, until onion is loose. Oust skillet from the warmth and blend in arugula and salt and pepper to taste. Brains flour tortillas on two warming sheets and top with arugula mix and Parmesan. Warmth pizzas on upper and lower racks of oven, trading spots of getting ready sheets almost through warming, until edges are splendid, around 10 minutes.

BACON CHEESEBURGER UPSIDE-DOWN PIZZA YIELD:

Ingredients:

1) 1-pound lean ground meat
2) One medium onion, quartered, cut
3) One medium ring pepper, chop into diminished down strips six cuts bacon, crisp-cooked
4) 1 (14 1/2 ounce) can thick pizza sauce 3 Italian plum tomatoes
5) Six cuts cheddar

Method:

Warmth grill to 400 degrees F.
In a large pot, a dull shaded ground burger with onion and ringer pepper; channel. Blend in 6 cuts broke down bacon and pizza sauce. Spoon into ungreased 13 x 9-inch getting ready to dish. Sprinkle consistently with tomatoes; top with cheddar cuts.

Beating two eggs

1 cup milk

One tablespoon oil

1 cup all-around convenient flour 1/4 teaspoon salt

Two slices bacon, crisp-cooked and broke down.

In a medium bowl, beat eggs insignificantly. Incorporate milk and oil; mix well. Carefully spoon flour into evaluating cup; level off. Incorporate flour and salt; beat 2 minutes at medium speed. Pour consistently over cheddar cuts. Sprinkle with broke down bacon. Warmth at 400 degrees F for 20 to 30 minutes or until fixing is somewhat puffed and significant splendid darker.

* 1/2-pound ground meat
* 1 little onion, hacked
* 1 pre-arranged Italian bread chill outside layer
* 8 ounces would pizza have the option to the sauce
* 6 bacon strips, cooked and crumbled
* 20 dill pickle coin cuts
* 2 cups devastated mozzarella cheddar
* 2 cups devastated cheddar
* 1 teaspoon pizza or Italian seasonings

In a skillet, cook cheeseburger and onion until meat isn't, now pink and channel by then put in a protected spot. Spot covering on an ungreased 12-inch pizza dish. Spread sauce, top with burger mix, bacon, pickles and cheeses; sprinkle with seasonings. Warmth at 450 for 10 minutes or until cheeses have mellowed. Cut into cuts and serve.

BACON ONION AND TOMATO PIZZA RECIPE:

Ingredients:

1) One tablespoon olive oil
2) One tablespoon of oil to brush the pita
3) 2 cups cut onions
4) Salt and pepper to taste
5) Three tablespoons darker sugar
6) 4 Greek-style pita pieces of bread (at any rate six sneaks in separation over)
7) Garlic powder to taste
8) 1/2 cup mozzarella cheddar
9) Two gigantic tomatoes washed, cut 1/4-inch-thick, split at whatever point needed
10) 1 1/2 cup cut fresh spinach, optional
11) 8 cups cooked bacon, each chop down the center, secluded
12) A cup of cheddar cheese

Directions:

Preheat the oven to 400 degrees. Incorporate the cut onions and season with salt and pepper. Sauté the onions until fragile, around 3 to 5 minutes. Sprinkle with the dark shaded sugar and continue cooking until the onions turn a splendid darker.

Remove from the glow and put it in a sheltered spot. Recognize the pita bread on a getting ready sheet and brush each with a thin covering of olive oil. Sprinkle each with the garlic powder and subsequently around two tablespoons of the mozzarella cheddar. Top with a touch of the onions and a short time later coordinate the tomato cuts on the pita. At whatever point needed, beautify with a bit of the spinach in the canter. Sort out four bacon cuts on top. Warmth around 8 to 10 minutes or until the tomatoes begin to smooth. Oust from the stove and sprinkle each with 1/4 cup of the cheddar. Return to the oven and warmth until the cheddar disintegrates. Oust from the grill and serve.

BACON SPINACH PIZZA RECIPE:

Ingredients:

* 1 can (10-oz. size) Refrigerated Pizza Crust
* 1 pack (9-oz. size) Chopped Frozen Spinach
* 1 tablespoon oil
* 1/2 cup coarsely severed onion
* 1 pack (6-oz. size) refrigerated cooked Italian-style chicken chest strips, divided
* 2 cups crushed mozzarella cheddar
* 1 pack (2.8 to 3-oz. size) precooked bacon cuts, cut into 1/2-INCH pieces

Method:

Warmth oven to 400°F. Oil 15X10X1-INCH warming holder. Unroll hitter; place in the lobed holder. Starting at canter, press out hitter to edge of skillet. Get ready at 400°F. for 9 to 13 minutes or until edges are light splendid dull shaded.

Meanwhile, cook spinach as facilitated in the group. Channel well; press to oust liquid. Warmth oil in a little skillet over medium-high warmth until hot. Incorporate onion; cook and blend 3 to 4 minutes or until fragile, mixing intermittently. Oust somewhat arranged structure from the grill. Top body with spinach, onion, chicken, cheddar, and bacon. Return to stove; set up an additional 9 to 12 minutes or until cheddar is broken down. Cut into squares.

ARRANGED PIZZA SANDWICH RECIPE:

Ingredients:

* 1-pound Lean Ground Beef
* 15 ounces Tomato Sauce
* 15 ounces Pizza Sauce
* 1 teaspoon Oregano Leaves
* 1 Egg
* 2/3 cup Milk
* 8 ounces Cheese
* 2 ounces Mushrooms
* 1/4 cup Parmesan Cheese; Grated

Directions:
* Use one 8-oz heap of cut strategy American or mozzarella cheddar.
Warmth the stove to 400 degrees F. Cook and blend the meat in a large skillet until dull hued. Direct off the wealth fat. Blend in half of the tomato sauce, and the oregano leaves into the meat mix. Warmth to rising by then decline the glow and stew, uncovered, for 10 minutes. While the meat mix is stewing, mix the planning mix, egg, and milk. Measure out 3/4 cup of the player and put it in a sheltered spot. Spread the remainder of the hitter in a lobed, getting ready compartment 9 X 9 X 2-INCHES. Spreading similarly. Layer 4 cups of the cheddar, the meat mix, the mushrooms, and the remainder of the cheddar on the tomato sauce. Spoon the held player on the most noteworthy purpose of the cheddar. Sprinkle the player top with the ground Parmesan cheddar and plan, uncovered until it is splendid dull shaded, 20 to 25 minutes. Cool for 5 minutes before cutting into squares and serving.

CHEESEBURGER TORTILLA PIZZA RECIPE:

Ingredients:

* 1-pound lean ground cheeseburger
* 1 medium onion - cut
* 1 teaspoon dried oregano leaves
* 1 teaspoon salt
* 4 tremendous (10 inch) flour tortillas
* 1 medium tomato - seeded and cut
* 1 tablespoon fresh basil leaves - gently cut
* 1 cup Mozzarella cheddar
* 1/4 cup Parmesan cheddar - ground

Methods:

Warmth grill to 400ºF. Dull shaded ground cheeseburger and onion in a skillet over medium warmth 8 to 10 minutes or until meat isn't, now pink. Pour off drippings. Blend oregano and salt into the meat.

Delicately brush tortillas with oil. Plan tortillas on two huge warming sheets in 400ºF oven for 3 minutes. Spoon cheeseburger mix consistently over top of each tortilla; top with a comparable proportion of tomato. Sprinkle with basil and cheeses. Return to grill and warmth 12 to 14 minutes or until tortillas are gently sung.

BREAKFAST PIZZA RECIPE:

Ingredients:

* 1/2-pound hotdog, cooked
* 1 bundle Crescent rolls
* 5 eggs
* 1/4 teaspoon dry mustard
* 1/4 teaspoon pepper
* 1/4 cup milk
* 1 cup ground cheddar

Methods:

Preheat stove to 375F. Oil an 8"x8" or 9"x9" container. Unfurl Crescent folds into strips and press together on base and sides. Whisk eggs, milk, mustard, and pepper. Sprinkle the frankfurter and potatoes, at that point the cheddar on Crescent rolls. Pour egg blend overall. Sprinkle with Parmesan cheddar. Prepare 40-45 minutes until no fluid in focus.

BROCCOLI TURKEY PIZZA RECIPE:

Ingredients:

* 1/3 cup low fat mayonnaise
* 1 tablespoon mustard
* 1/2 teaspoon pepper
* 2 1/2 cups cleaved crisp or defrosted solidified broccoli
* 2 cups cubed cooked turkey
* 1 cup cheddar
* 1 (12-inch size) round Boboli

Method:

In a medium bowl, consolidate mayonnaise, Dionisio, and pepper. Mix in broccoli, turkey, and cheddar. Spread turkey blend on the outside layer and prepare at 425F for 12 minutes or until gently seared.

AIR POCKET PIZZA RECIPE:

Ingredients:

* 1 1/2-pound meat, caramelized
* 15 ounces pizza sauce
* 1 can refrigerated buttermilk scones
* 12 ounces pizza mix cheddar

Bearings:

Add pizza sauce to ground meat. Cut bread rolls in quarters and spot in a lobed 9X13 dish. Top with hamburger blend. Prepare at 400F degrees for 20 minutes. Sprinkle with cheddar and prepare until cheddar liquefies. Let stand 5-10 minutes before serving. You can include your preferred garnishes alongside the meat before heating.

* three bundles (7.5-ounce size) buttermilk rolls
* 1 container (14-ounce size) spaghetti sauce
* 3 cups mozzarella cheddar, separated
* 1 colossal clove garlic, slashed fine

Preheat stove to 350 degrees. Quarter bread rolls utilizing kitchen shears and spot in a medium-sized bowl. Mix in 1 cup of sauce, 2 cups of cheddar, and the garlic. Include whatever fixings you like and blend to consolidate. Spread blend in a lobed 9-by-13 container. Pour remaining sauce and cheddar over the top. Prepare for 30-35 minutes.

BUTTERNUT SQUASH, BACON, AND ROSEMARY PIZZA RECIPE:

Ingredients:

* 1 1/2-pound butternut squash
* 1 tablespoon vegetable oil
* 1/2 cup water
* 6 tablespoons unsalted margarine, liquefied and kept warm
* ten sheets phyllo stacked between sheets of wax paper and secured with a kitchen towel
* 9 tablespoons parmesan cheddar - ground
* 6 cuts bacon cut into 1/2-INCH pieces
* 1 tablespoon crisp rosemary leaves - minced
* 6 scallion greens - slashed
* 1 small red onion, cut into pieces

Directions:

Quarter squash the long way and dispose of seeds. Strip squash cautiously and cut into 3/4-inch pieces. In a sizeable overwhelming skillet cook squash in oil over moderate warmth, mixing every so often, 2 minutes.

Add water and salt to taste and stew, secured, until squash is merely delicate, around 10 minutes. Stew squash, revealed until practically all water is vanished, around 5 minutes. In a nourishment processor, purée squash with salt and pepper to taste. Squash purée might be made one day ahead and chilled, secured. Preheat grill to 400°F. Softly brush an enormous preparing sheet with some spread and put one sheet phyllo on margarine. Gently brush phyllo with some outstanding spread and sprinkle with one tablespoon Parmesan. Put another sheet of phyllo over cheddar, squeezing it immovably with the goal that it clings to the base layer. Spread, sprinkle with cheddar, and layer remaining phyllo in a similar way, finishing with a sheet of phyllo. Delicately brush top sheet with outstanding margarine.

Overlap in all sides 1/4 inch, squeezing to top sheet, and overlay up a 1/4-inch fringe, pleating corners. Spread squash purée uniformly on phyllo outside layer and top with bacon, rosemary, scallion greens, and onion. Heat pizza in the canter of the appliance until the outside layer is brilliant, around 15 minutes.

CAMPER'S PIZZA RECIPE:

Ingredients:

* 12 ounces ground hamburger - 80% lean
* 1 medium onion
* 1/2 teaspoon salt
* 8 ounces refrigerated bow rolls
* 8 ounces pizza sauce
* 4 ounces mushroom stems and pieces - slashed
* 2 1/4 ounces ready olives - hollowed and cut
* 1/3 cup green chime pepper - coarsely hacked
* 4 ounces Mozzarella cheddar
* 1 teaspoon dried oregano leaves

Method:

Cook ground meat and onion in all around prepared 11 to 12-INCH overwhelming skillet with heat-verification handle over medium coals* until not, at this point pink, mixing periodically to separate hamburger. Expel hamburger blend to paper towel; season with salt. Pour off drippings, leaving skillet "lobed." Separate bow moves mixture triangles; place in skillet, squeezing edges together to frame base outside layer and 1-inch edge up the side of skillet. A spread portion of pizza sauce over batter; spoon ground hamburger blend over the sauce.

Top with mushrooms, olives, and ringer pepper. Pour remaining sauce over all; sprinkle with cheddar and oregano. Spot skillet in the focus of lattice over medium coals.

CANADIAN BACON PIZZA RECIPE

Ingredients:

* 1 (12 inch) pizza covering - unbaked
* 1 cup pizza sauce
* 2/3 cup mozzarella cheddar
* 6 ounces Canadian bacon - cut in bits
* 1/2 cup meagrely cut crisp mushrooms
* 1 little green or red ringer pepper - cut in rings
* 1/2 teaspoon squashed dried oregano
* 1/2 teaspoon squashed dried basil
* crushed red pepper drops

Method:

Preheat grill to 450F. Spot the unbaked pizza covering on an ungreased non-stick pizza dish. Spread the pizza sauce over the outside layer, leaving a 1-inch fringe around the edge. Sprinkle with half of the cheddar. Orchestrate the Canadian bacon on the cheddar, covering uniformly. Top with mushroom cuts and chime pepper rings.

Sprinkle equitably with oregano, basil, and red pepper pieces. Top with outstanding cheddar. Heat for 13 to 15 minutes, until the outside layer is fresh and the cheddar is dissolved and seared.

BACON PIZZA RECIPE:

Ingredients:

* 2 tablespoons margarine
* 2 medium pears, cored, each cut into 12 the long way cuts
* 2 tablespoons solidly pressed dark colored sugar
* 4 singular pizza outside layers (8 inches)
* 1/2 cup alfredo sauce
* 1 cup mozzarella cheddar
* 3/4 cup disintegrated blue cheddar
* 3/4 cup bacon bits (genuine)

Method:

Liquefy spread in medium skillet on medium warmth. Include pears; sprinkle uniformly with dark-colored sugar. Cook 2 to 3 minutes or until sugar is softened, and pears are equally covered, mixing every so often. Expel skillet from heat; put in a safe spot Spread every pizza outside layer with 2 Tbsp. Alfredo sauce; top each with layers of 1/4 cup of the mozzarella cheddar, 3 Tbsp. of the blue cheddar, 3 Tbsp. of the bacon, and six pear cuts. Spot on the heating sheet. Heat at 425 F for 6 to 8 minutes or until garnish is brilliant and bubbly.

PANCETTA PIZZA RECIPE:

Ingredients:

* 1 cup warm water (105 degrees)
* 1 1/4-ounce bundle yeast
* 3 cups generally useful flour
* 1 teaspoon salt
* 1 teaspoon sugar
* 2 tablespoons olive oil
* 2 onions
* 2 teaspoons olive oil
* 1 1/2 teaspoon salt
* 1 1/2 cup coarsely ground fontina
* 6 cuts pancetta, cooked until fresh
* 1 clove garlic, cut down the middle
* 1 shower of olive oil
* salt and pepper to taste

Method:

Empty the water into a large bowl. Sprinkle in the yeast and sugar and mix to break down. Let it remain until the blend starts to bubble. This should take around 5 minutes. Begin it once again with another bundle of yeast.

Mix in 1 cup of flour, the salt, and one tablespoon olive oil. Blend in with a wooden spoon until altogether consolidated. Include the rest of the flour 1/2 cup at once, blending after every expansion.

On a daintily floured surface, manipulate mixture until smooth and versatile, around 10 minutes. Oil an enormous bowl with the staying olive oil. Spot batter in an oiled bowl spread with saran wrap and a warm drying towel, and let the mixture ascend in a warm spot until multiplied in mass. This will take 1 to 1/2 hours.

Punch down the mixture and return it to the floured surface. Gap mixture into two balls and spread each with cling wrap, leaving space for development. Permit to twofold in size once more. Caramelized Onions: Heat oil in enormous non-stick salute containers over medium warmth. Include meagrely cut onions and season with salt; saute 5 minutes. Diminish warmth to medium-low. Mix now and again to get a smooth shading. Cook until extremely delicate and a rich, brilliant shading creates, around 20 minutes longer. Cool somewhat. Preheat grill to 475 degrees. Turn out two batter circles on a softly floured surface to 8-inch adjusts. Sprinkle two heating sheets or pizza stones with cornmeal. Rub a liberal shower of olive oil on the batter. Rub raw garlic clove all over the mixture. Top with fontina, caramelized onions, and pancetta. Season with salt and pepper. Heat pizza for 10-12 minutes, until foaming and fresh.

CHEDDAR STEAK PIZZA RECIPE:

Ingredients:

* 1 arranged pizza outside (12 inches)
* 1/2 cup grill sauce or pizza sauce
* 1 bundle (6 oz.) Grilled Beef Steak Strips
* 2 cups Shredded Cheese
* Sliced green pepper and onion

Method:

Spread pizza outside with grill sauce. Top with meat steak strips, cheddar, green pepper, and onion. Spot on the treated sheet. Heat at 450 F for 8 to 10 minutes or until cheddar is liquefied.

* 1 (10 oz. size) slight pre-prepared pizza shell
* 4 ounces cream cheddar
* 3/4 teaspoon Italian flavoring
* 1/4 teaspoon crisply ground pepper
* 2 cups leaf lettuce
* 1 cup finely Co-Jack cheddar
* 3/4 cup cleaved new tomato
* 7 cuts bacon, cooked until fresh, cleaved
* olives, cut (discretionary)

Directions:

Preheat grill to 400 degrees. Spot pizza shell on the prepared sheet. Warmth in grill 5 minutes or until somewhat fresh. Expel from the stove and let cool marginally. Join cream cheddar, Italian flavoring, and pepper. Spread on pizza shell to inside 1/2 inch of edge. Sprinkle with lettuce, Co-Jack cheddar, tomato, and bacon. Top with sliced olives whenever wanted. Cut pizza into wedges and serve.

MUSHY JALAPENO AND EGG PIZZA RECIPE:

Ingredients:

*   6 eggs
*   6 cups cheddar
*   6 cups mozzarella cheddar
*   6 ounces cut jalapenos
*   Pepperoni, cut

Method:

Blend eggs, cheddar, and jalapenos. Fill rectangular goulash. Lay cuts of pepperoni on top and spot into 350-degree F stove. Cook until cheddar is brilliant (around 10-15 minutes). Let represent 5 minutes, cut into 2-INch squares, and serve.

Preheated stove to 475. Blend the above ingredients for 10 minutes in a robust blender or manipulate by hand. Presently include 2 1/2 cups of flour. Blend for 15 minutes in a robust blender with a battered snare or by hand. Presently the mixture must ascent. The batter ought to be in a massive bowl in a warm spot, secured with a drying towel.

If it isn't warm in the kitchen, turn the stove on to the least setting (close to 100) and let the mixture ascend in the bowl in the appliance, secured by the towel. Let ascend just because (about 60 minutes) and punch down the batter. Let rise once more, punch down, and use. Push the battery out level with your fingers, in a high-sided pizza container, or a sizeable dark iron skillet. Spread with mozzarella cheddar. Spread with tomato sauce with Italian herbs and flavors included. Spread with hacked garlic, green peppers, cut pepperoni, sweet Italian sausage, cut mushrooms, cleaned onions, or whatever to taste. Sprinkle with ground Romano or Parmesan cheddar. Cook in a grill at 475 until done, around 15 to 20 minutes relying upon garnishes and thickness of the outside layer and how fresh you need it cooked.

CIRO'S PIZZA RECIPE:

Ingredients:

*   1/2-pound flour
*   1/2-ounce pastry specialists' yeast
*   1 tablespoon water to mix yeast
*   1 tablespoon olive oil, in addition to extra to hose pizza at the end
*   Salt and pepper
*   1 egg
*   1/4 cup high temp water
*   2 jars (1 pound 12-OUNCE) crisp egg-molded tomatoes, cleaned, seeded and generally slashed
*   2 teaspoons escapades
*   1/2 little tin anchovies in oil, depleted
*   5 cuts mozzarella cheddar
*   ten dark olive pants
*   1 sprig oregano
*   1 little garlic clove, finely cut
*   Freshly ground dark pepper, for decorating

Method:

Spot the flour in a bowl. Make a well in the inside, add the yeast blended to glue with water, and afterward the olive oil, salt, pepper, and egg. Combine and afterward slim glue with boiling water until it looks like biting gum and leaves from the hands.

Manipulate for around 3 minutes until it no longer sticks to hands. Shape batter into a ball spread with a bowl and permit to stand 30 minutes. Massage again and afterward get the mixture and haul it out with the fingers, turning it around. Oil a heating sheet and preheat broiler to 500 degrees F. Spot the batter onto the heating sheet, spreading it out to frame 12-inch breadth round shape. The edge ought to be somewhat thicker than the middle. Enhancement with tomatoes, escapades, anchovies, mozzarella cheddar, dark olive parts, oregano leaves, garlic, and pepper. Sprinkle with oil and spot into the stove for 20 minutes. Spot on serving dish.

CLUB PIZZA RECIPE:

Ingredients:

* 1 prebaked slim Italian pizza outside layer
* 10 ounces arranged Alfredo sauce
* 10 ounces hacked solidified spinach - defrosted
* 1 cup cubed cooked chicken
* 1 cup hacked tomato
* 6 cuts bacon - cooked

Method:

Warmth stove to 450F degrees. Spot pizza outside layer in a large ungreased treat sheet. Spread hull with Alfredo sauce. Top with spinach, chicken, tomato, and bacon. Prepare at 450F degrees for 8 to 10 minutes or until thoroughly warmed.

In a little bowl, consolidate cream cheddar, mayonnaise, and horseradish sauce and mix well. Spread over the pizza covering. Top with ham, plum tomatoes, and lettuce and sprinkle with a plate of mixed greens dressing. Cut into wedges and serve right away.

CORNCAKE PIZZA WHEELS RECIPE:

Ingredients:

* 1-pound ground meat
* 1 can (16-ounce size) kidney beans, washed
* 1 can (8-ounce size) tomato sauce
* 4 teaspoons bean stew powder
* 1 container (4-ounce size) diced paprika
* 1 can (4-ounce size) cleaved green chilies
* 1 cup cheddar
* 2 tablespoons cornmeal
* 2 tubes (11-1/2-ounce size) refrigerated corncake turns
* Shredded lettuce, cut tomatoes, and acrid cream

Method:

In a skillet, cook the hamburger over medium warmth until not, at this point, pink; channel. Include the beans, tomato sauce, and stew powder. Stew revealed until the liquid has dissipated. Expel from the warmth and cold. Mix in the pimientos, chilies, and cheddar; put in a safe spot. Sprinkle two-lobed 14-IN. Pizza dish with corn-dinner. Pat the hoecake batter into a 14-IN. Hover on each dish. With a blade, cut a 7-in. X in the canter of the batter. Cut another 7-in. X to frame eight pie-formed wedges in the middle. Spoon the filling around the edge of the mixture. Overlay purposes of batter over filling; fold under the ring and squeeze to seal (filling will be noticeable). Heat at 400F for 15-20 minutes or until brilliant dark-colored. Fill focus with lettuce, tomatoes, and harsh cream.

CORN TORTILLA PIZZAS RECIPE

Ingredients:

* 1 1/4-pound ground burger
* 1 little onion, sliced
* 1/2 cup sliced green pepper
* 3 containers (6-ounce size) tomato stick
* 1 1/4 cup water
* 1 cup salsa
* 2 cups fresh or hardened corn
* 1 1/2 cup cut new tomatoes
* 3/4 cup cut prepared olives
* 1 envelope taco enhancing
* 3 teaspoons garlic powder
* 1 1/2 teaspoon dried parsley drops
* 1/2 teaspoon dried oregano
* 1/8 teaspoon salt
* 1/4 teaspoon pepper
* 32 corn or flour tortillas (6-inch size)
* 8 cups obliterated mozzarella cheddar

Method:

In a skillet, cook cheeseburger, onion, and green pepper over medication. Heat until meat isn't, now pink; channel. In a bowl, merge tomato pastes and water until blended; incorporate salsa. Blend into meat corn, tomatoes, olives, and seasonings. Spot tortillas on ungreased warming sheets. Spread each with 1/4 cup meat mix to inside 1/2 inch of edge and sprinkle with 1/4 cup of cheddar. Warmth at 375F for 5-7 minutes or until mellowed.

CRAZY CRUST PIZZA RECIPE:

Ingredients:

* 1 cup flour
* 1 teaspoon salt
* 1 teaspoon Italian seasoning or oregano
* 1/8 teaspoon pepper
* 2 eggs
* 2/3 cup milk Topping
* 1-pound ground burger/sausage
* 1 cup pepperoni
* 1/4 cup sliced onion
* 1 cup pizza sauce
* 8 ounces tomato sauce mixed in with oregano and pepper
* 1 cup wrecked Mozzarella cheddar
* 1 can (4 oz.) mushrooms

Directions:

In medium skillet darker ground meat, seasoning to taste. (No convincing motivation to darker pepperoni). Channel well, put in a sheltered spot. Tenderly oil and build-up 12- or 14-inch pizza skillet or 10X15 jam move dish with flour or corn supper. Plan hitter by mixing to flour, salt, Italian enhancing, pepper, eggs, and milk in a touch of mixing bowl. Pour hitter in skillet, tilting dish, so player covers the base. Compose fixing of meat and onions over the player. Warmth on-base rack in a 425-degree oven for 20-25 minutes or until pizza is significant splendid dim shaded. Oust from stove; shower with pizza sauce and sprinkle with cheddar. Top with mushrooms or various toppings. Return to the stove for 10-15 minutes until cheddar is melted and sauce is bubbly.

CRAZY CRUST PIZZA II RECIPE:

Ingredients:

* 1 cup flour
* 3 eggs
* 2/3 cup milk
* 1/2-pound ground meat
* 1/2 cup onions
* Pizza sauce
* Cheese
* Pepperoni
* Mushrooms
* Bell pepper
* Onions

Method:

Mix flour, eggs, and milk. Beat 2 to 3 minutes. Dull shaded ground cheeseburger and onions. Oil getting ready sheet; pour flour mix onto the sheet. Incorporate meat and onions. Warmth for 25 minutes at 425 degrees F. Remove from grill. Incorporate sauce, cheddar, and remaining ingredients. Set up an additional 10 minutes.

Dull shaded meat and pepper together and channel oil. Prepare a player and fill a lubed pizza dish. Tilt holder, so the player covers the base. Genius meat mix, onion, and mushrooms over the hitter.

Get ready at 425 for 20 minutes or until splendid darker. Oust from the stove and incorporate pizza sauce and cheddar. Return to the stove for ten extra minutes or until cheddar mellow. Detect a square of foil on a treat sheet. Put the burger mix on the foil. Pat out the meat entirely into a 10-inch float around 1/2 inch thick. Build up a standing edge around 1-inch high all around the edge of the circle. This makes a meat "frame" for your pizza (make sure to make the meat edge adequately high and firm enough so it will thwart the meat crushes and soup sauce from ascending over). Turn up the edges of the foil to get drippings. Spread the rest of the ten 3/4-ounce container of tomato soup over meat. Top cheeseburger outside layer with Mozzarella cheddar and more oregano and mushrooms. Warmth at 450 degrees for 15 minutes or until done.

STRAIGHTFORWARD BAKE OVEN DEEP DISH PIZZA RECIPE:

Ingredients:

* 2 tablespoons for the most part valuable flour
* 1/8 teaspoon getting the ready powder
* Dash of salt
* 1 teaspoon margarine
* 2 1/4 teaspoons milk
* 1 tablespoon pizza sauce
* 1 1/2 tablespoon demolished mozzarella cheddar

Directions:

Combine flour, getting ready powder, salt and margarine until blend seems like medium-sized pieces. Bit by bit incorporate milk while blending. Shape hitter into a ball and spot into a lobed compartment. Use your fingers to pat the blend similarly over the base of the holder, by then up the sides. Pour the sauce similarly over the hitter by then sprinkle with the cheddar. Get ready 20 mins. Oust. Make the French Bread blend recipe on any occasion one day as of now in case you can. Transform the blend out into the condition of a pizza, put it on a pizza dish, and put it in a sheltered spot. It will keep in the more relaxed present moment. Set up the dried mushrooms as showed by conveyed plans (douse, wash, cut, resoak, wash, channel). If the snails are unnecessarily enormous (more significant than a garlic clove), then cut them in pieces. Channel the snails well. Mellow the spread in a warming dish, incorporate the snails, squashed garlic, around 1/2 salt, and ground dull pepper to taste.

Put the bread-hitter compartment on the top rack of the stove and the snails on the base rack of the oven, and cook them both for 10 minutes. Take them out. Spread the tomato sauce in an even layer on the bread, by then sprinkle the Raclette cheddar over it. Incorporate the snails, and a while later, the mushrooms. Sprinkle with new parmesan cheddar, salt, and pepper. Get ready at 425 degrees F. in the top rack for 12 minutes (base rack will devour the frame). Get it, use fondue cheddar or a Gruyere.

FIG AND PROSCIUTTO PIZZA RECIPE:

Ingredients:

*   1 group dynamic dry yeast, that has reliably been in a cooler
*   1 contact of sugar
*   3/4 cup warm water, not any more sizzling than 110 (from the tap)
*   3 cups commonly helpful flour
*   2 tablespoons olive oil
*   2 teaspoons sea salt
*   Olive oil for the resting bowl Pizza
*   1 half quart new figs, stems ousted, slice to the thickness of a pea.
*   1/2-pound Prosciutto di Parma from San Daniele.
*   1 tablespoon fennel seeds
*   Extra virgin olive oil
*   pizza player

Method:

For Pizza Dough: "Start" the yeast by mixing it in with the sugar and water for around seven to ten minutes. Put the yeast, sugar and water mix in your remarkable blender, fitted with the blend catch. Incorporate the flour, olive oil, and salt. Start the machine and let mix until a blend ball structures. Stop the machine and let the hitter rest for three minutes. Heartbeat the machine on numerous occasions. Flour on the counter and put the blend on the floured surface. Handle for five minutes.

Coat a medium-sized bowl with some olive oil. Put the player in the bowl, by then turn the blend over, so the different sides are made sure about with a film of oil. Spread the bowl with cling wrap. Put the bowl in a warm spot for 2 hours so the blend can rise. Following two hours, punch the hitter from the inside to level. Put it on a floured counter. Chop the player down the canter, and freeze one half for at some point later. Crease the other half into a ball and spread it with the bowl for thirty minutes.

For Fig and Prosciutto Pizza: Toast the fennel seeds in a hot, dry dish around five minutes. Put in a sheltered spot. Warmth your oven to 4750 with a pizza stone on the most raised rack. Use a treat sheet dish that has no edges. Spread it well with Wonda flour or cornmeal. Uncover the blend to the size of the pizza stone.

Move the blend onto the floured sheet dish. Spread out a layer of prosciutto, by then the figs, on the blend. Sprinkle the pizza with the toasted fennel. Move the pizza to the pizza stone by putting the sheet compartment on the stone and quickly pulling the plate away, so the pizza slides.

Warmth for five minutes or until the base of the outside is splendid darker. Oust the pizza from the stone by using the sheet dish and a significant spatula. Not sometime before serving, put the pizza onto a cutting load up. Shower it well with the extra virgin olive oil and cut it into squares.

NEW TOMATO AND BASIL PIZZA RECIPE:

Ingredients:

*   1 (12") Italian bread shell-like Boboli
*   1 tablespoon olive oil
*   1/2 cup ground or Parmesan cheddar, isolated
*   3 plum tomatoes, cut
*   1/4 teaspoon ground dark pepper
*   2 tablespoons crisp basil

Method:

Preheat grill to 450F. Brush bread shell with olive oil. Sprinkle 1/4 cup of the cheddar over the hull. Top with tomato cuts and staying 1/4 cup cheddar. Sprinkle with pepper. Prepare straightforwardly on broiler rack for 8-10 minutes or until the covering is fresh and cheddar is dissolved. Sprinkle with basil before serving.

GLUTEN-FREE RICE CRUST PIZZA RECIPE:

Ingredients:

* 2 1/2 cups cooked white rice
* 1/4 cup mozzarella cheddar, ground
* 1 egg, delicately beaten
* 1/4 cup onion, finely hacked
* 1 clove garlic, minced
* 1 teaspoon olive oil
* 1 tablespoon margarine, liquefied
* 1 cup tomato sauce or pizza sauce
* 1/2 teaspoon oregano or basil, dried
* 3/4 cup mozzarella cheddar, ground
* 1/4 cup Parmesan or asiago cheddar

Method:

Preheat stove to 425 degrees F. Blends the initial four ingredients completely. Spread equally on the base of a 12-inch pizza container or pie dish. Prepare 15 minutes or until the surface is delicately dark-colored. Sauté onion and garlic in the olive oil. Spread over the hull. Spread on the pizza sauce; include dry herbs if the sauce is flat. Sprinkle on the two sorts of cheddar. Come back to the grill and prepare for 8-10 minutes until the sauce is bubbly, and the cheddar is softened.

GOAT CHEESE AND WALNUT PIZZA RECIPE:

Ingredients:

* 1 pizza hull
* 6 ounces Fresh goat cheddar
* 2 tablespoons Walnut or safflower oil
* 1/2 cup Walnuts

Method:

Disintegrate the goat cheddar and sprinkle it everywhere throughout the pizza. In a little bowl hurl, the pecans with the pecan or safflower oil to cover. Spot the pecans everywhere throughout the pizza. Heat as per headings. Spread goat cheddar on pizza shell Sprinkle garlic, basil, salt, and pepper over cheddar Spread out tomatoes and mushrooms Sprinkle with olive oil Let rest for five minutes prior.

CHICAGO-STYLE DEEP-DISH PIZZA RECIPE:

Ingredients:

* 1 bundle quick ascent active yeast (1/4 oz.)
* 1 cup warm water, between 105-115ºF
* 1 teaspoon sugar
* 1 teaspoon sugar
* 2 1/2 cups flour
* 1/2 cup yellow cornmeal
* 1/4 cup olive oil
* 1 pound mozzarella cheddar
* 1-pound cooked Italian hotdog
* 1 (28 oz.) can diced tomatoes
* 1 teaspoon dried sweet basil
* 1 teaspoon dried oregano
* 1/2 cup ground Parmesan cheddar

Method:

In the blending bowl includes the warm water, yeast, and sugar, mix with a whisk. Include 2 cups of the flour, salt, cornmeal, and olive oil. Utilize the oar and blend on speed 2 for 2 minutes. Put on the batter snare and include the rest of the flour. Manipulate on speed two until the batter sticks to the snare, and afterward massage on speed 2 for 5 minutes longer. Spot the batter in a lobed bowl and spread. Let ascend for 60 minutes. With oiled fingers, press the mixture into a deep-dish pizza skillet. Spread the mixture with the mozzarella, and afterward top with the meat. Spot the tomatoes over the hotdog. Top with the basil, oregano, and Parmesan cheddar. Heat in a 500ºF grill for 15 minutes. Diminish the warmth to 350ºF and prepare for 20 minutes, or until the hull is dark-colored

BRILLIANT GATE PIZZA RECIPE:

Ingredients:

* 1 (12-to 14-INCH size) pizza outside layer
* 1 cup cheddar,
* 1/2-pound crisp mozzarella (water-free), 1/4-inch cuts
* 1/2 cup pizza sauce
* 1 cup Italian salami, cut into rounds or strips
* 1 cup pepperoni, thinly cut into rounds or strips

Directions:

Preheat grill to 425 degrees F. Spread the pizza sauce on the somewhat prepared outside layer. Sprinkle Cheddar equally over the sauce. Mastermind salami, frankfurter, and pepperoni uniformly over Cheddar. Top pizza with mozzarella cuts. Heat around 15 minutes or until cheddar is dissolved, and the outside layer is fresh and brilliant. Join ground meat, salt, and pepper. Pat meat into 9-inch nonstick pie skillet. Spread tomatoes over meat. Consolidate remaining ingredients; sprinkle over tomato-meat blend. Heat at 350 degrees for 20 minutes. Slice into six equal wedges to serve. String the string cheddar into slight steps. Spread two tablespoons of pizza sauce on each shell. Sprinkle 1/2 cup of the cheddar on each bread shells Arrange pepperoni or olives on every pizza to make a grinning face. Heat 10 to 14 minutes or until cheddar is softened.

HAWTHORNE LANE'S PEPPERONI PIZZA RECIPE:

Ingredients:

* 2 pc. Pizza mixture (see beneath)
* 1 teaspoon Virgin olive oil
* 2 cups Whole milk mozzarella cheddar, ground (inexactly pressed)
* 1/2 cup Buffalo mozzarella, cubed into 1/2" pieces (around 4 oz.)
* 1 Red ringer pepper, simmered, stripped and cut into 1/4" strips
* 12 Kalamata olives
* 2 tablespoons Grated Parmesan cheddar
* 2 ounces Gingras Family Smoked Pepperoni, cut meagrely (1/8" or less)
* 2 tablespoons Chopped Italian parsley Pizza Dough
* 4 cups All reason flour
* 1 1/2 cup warm water (around 90 F.)
* 1 teaspoon salt
* 1 teaspoon fresh yeast
* 1 1/2 teaspoon Honey
* 1 tablespoon Olive oil

Method:

Preheat the broiler to 500 F. what's more, place a preparing stone or tile in to warm. Fold the batters into about 10 " adjusts utilizing a pie pin or by beating and extending the mixture. Sprinkle a light cutting board or pizza strip with cornmeal or semolina and lay the batters down on it. Brush the olive oil over the focal point of the mixture at that point spread the mozzarella cheddar equally over the batter, leaving a half-inch edge without cheddar. Orchestrate the cubed wild ox mozzarella, the olives, and the simmered peppers over the cheddar.

At last, slide the pizzas into the stove. Prepare for five minutes at that point expel from the stove and mastermind the cut pepperoni over the cheddar and sprinkle the Parmesan over. Come back to them over and keep on preparing for five additional minutes or until the edge of the hull gets brilliant dark-colored, and the cheddar rises in the inside. Expel from the stove and spot on a cutting board. Sprinkle the cleaved Italian parsley over and cut into six or eight pieces. Serve right away. Pizza Dough makes batters for six pizzas Join the salt, flour, and nectar in an electric blender and blend utilizing the batter snare to disseminate equitably. Include the water and yeast and blend for two minutes at low speed to unite the mixture. Speed up to medium and blend for six minutes, pushing the batter over into the blending bowl on the off chance that it crawls up the side.

Include the olive oil and blend until the mixture has ingested to oil and returns together. Turn out onto a softly floured work surface and massage by hand to harden. Structure into a ball and permit to rest for 30 minutes under a sodden fabric. Scale into 4-1/2 oz. Pieces at that point structure into tight balls by moving under your hand.

Spot water, milk, sugar, salt, shortening, and olive oil in the bowl of nourishment processor and heartbeat to break down sugar and salt. Include yeast, semolina or corn supper, bread flour, and universally handy flour. Procedure until a delicate ball structure. Expel from the machine and permit to rest, secured with a towel, around 45 minutes. Or, on the other hand, to make by hand: Use just universally handy flour. Spot water, milk, sugar, salt, shortening, and olive oil in a bowl and break down sugar and salt. Mix in yeast, semolina or corn supper, generally useful flour and ply to shape a delicate, yet not a very clingy batter (8-10 minutes). Permit to rest, secured with a towel around 45 minutes.

Empty batter tenderly before utilizing and permit it to rest 15 minutes more before utilizing it in a formula. You may refrigerate the mixture in an oiled plastic pack for as long as two days. Shape mixture into a heart. Top with your preferred sauce and fixings. Prepare in a hot grill 425 - 450°F. for 15 - 20 minutes. Trim the pizza shell(s) or focaccia bread into a heart shape, place on pizza skillet, or heating sheet. Spread pizza sauce on the shell to approach the edge. Sprinkle cheddar over the sauce, not precisely to edge of sauce. Spot shrimp, two by two, tails contacting, to make hearts, on cheddar. Do likewise with individual cuts of red ringer pepper, utilizing the top, where it bends, for the highest point of the heart. Put a couple of cuts of artichoke heart to a great extent. Shower a little olive oil over the top. Sprinkle with minced basil (discretionary).

Ingredients:

* 1 (10 oz.) pizza dough
* 4 teaspoons margarine
* 1/2 red pepper, cut
* 1 leek, cut into 1-INCH strips
* half of the boneless and skinless chicken breast, cut into little shapes
* 1/4 cup pesto
* artichoke hearts, coarsely slashed, to taste
* 4 ounces Fontina cheddar,
* 1/2 cup mozzarella cheddar,
* 1/2 teaspoon dried oregano

Method:

Preheat grill to 425°F. Unroll refrigerated pizza batter into square shape or square shape. Make a heart shape layout out of paper towels or cardboard. Spot format on batter and cut around heart shape utilizing scissors. Spot heart-molded batter on lobed treat sheet and adhere to guidelines on mixture can for prebaking pizza outside layer. Put hull in a safe spot. Sauté red pepper and leeks in half of the margarine until practically delicate. Expel from skillet. Include chicken and other portions of the spread to skillet and cook until chicken is done and gently seared.

Spread pesto over prebaked pizza outside layer. Top with sautéed leeks, red peppers, and chicken. Include artichoke hearts. Top with cheeses and prepare at 425°F. for 7 to 10 minutes. Sprinkle with oregano.

NATIVELY CONSTRUCTED PIZZA RECIPE:

Ingredients:

*   1 bundle Active Dry Yeast
*   1 cup Warm Water (105 to 115 degrees)
*   1 teaspoon Sugar
*   1 teaspoon salt
*   2 tablespoons Oil
*   2 1/2 cups Flour Sauce
*   1/2 cup slashed Onion
*   1 (8-oz.) would tomato be able to Sauce
*   1/4 teaspoon salt
*   1 1/8 teaspoon packaged Garlic, or more to taste
*   1/8 teaspoon White Pepper Meat and Vegetable Toppings
*   1 cup cut Pepperoni
*   1 cup slashed Onion
*   1 cup solidified Birdseye Stir-singed Peppers
*   1 (4oz.) can cut Mushrooms
*   1 cup cut Ripe Olives
*   1 pound Sweet or Hot Italian Sausage, expelled from housings

Mixture:

Break down yeast in warm water. Mix in unusual mixture ingredients. Beat enthusiastically, around 20 strokes. Spread bowl, permit the mixture to rest around 15 minutes, or until you have arranged sauce.

Sauce:

Blend sauce ingredients put in a safe spot. Warmth Oven to 425 degrees Separation batter into equal parts. On gently lobed 12" pizza dish sprinkled with a light covering of corn supper, pat every 50% of batter out into a 10 to 12-inch hover on pizza container. Separation sauce equally between pizza outside layers and spread out. Sprinkle every pizza with 1/4 cup Parmesan Cheese.

Sauté' frankfurter until nearly done, blending to separate. Include the peppers, onions, mushrooms, olives, and pepperoni and keep cooking until frankfurter is done. Dump the skillet brimming with cooked garnishes in a colander to deplete. Channel well overall. Sprinkle fixings equally onto the highest points of pizzas. Sprinkle 1 cup Mozzarella Cheese on every one of the pizzas. Prepare 20 to 25 minutes on the lower rack of the stove at 425 degrees until the hull is dark-colored and filling is hot and bubbly.

CUSTOM MADE PIZZA RECIPE:

Ingredients:

* one 1/4-ounce dynamic pastry specialist's yeast
* 1 teaspoon sugar
* 1 1/4 cup warm water (110-115 degrees)
* 1/4 cup vegetable oil
* 1 teaspoon salt
* 3 1/2 cups universally handy flour
* 1/2-pound ground hamburger
* 1 little onion
* 15 ounces tomato sauce
* 1 tablespoon dried oregano
* 1 teaspoon dried basil
* 1 medium green pepper
* 2 cups mozzarella cheddar

Directions:

An enormous bowl, disintegrate yeast and sugar in water; let represent 5 min. Include oil and salt. Mix in flour, a cup at once, to frame delicate mixture. Turn onto floured board; work until smooth and flexible, around 2-3 min. A spot in a lobed bowl, turning once to oil top. Spread and let ascend in a warm spot until multiplied, around 45 min.

In the interim, dark-colored meat and onion; channel. Punch mixture down; separate into equal parts. Press each into a lobed 12" pizza skillet. Consolidate the tomato sauce, oregano, and basil; spread over each outside layer. Top with hamburger blend, green pepper, and cheddar. Heat at 400 degrees for 25-30 minutes or until the outside layer is delicately caramelized.

* 1 (10-ounce size) round pre-prepared slender hull Italian bread shell

* 1 can (8-ounce size) pizza sauce

* 1 can (8-ounce size) can pineapple goodies in juice, all around depleted

* 1 bundle (6-ounce size) Canadian bacon cuts, quartered

* 2 tablespoons seeded jalapeño chiles (or to taste)

* 3/4 cup cheddar

* 3/4 cup mozzarella cheddar Directions:

Warmth broiler to 400°F. Spot bread shell on massive ungreased preparing sheet. Spread pizza sauce equally over shell; top with every residual fixing. Prepare for 8 to 10 minutes or until cheddar is dissolved and ingredients are warmed through. To serve, cut into wedges.

FRANK PIZZA RECIPE

Ingredients:

* 2 English biscuits, split
* 2 franks, each cut into 12 cuts
* 1/4 cup dense tomato soup
* 1/4 cup cheddar

Method:

Warmth grill to 350. Spot biscuit parts cut side up on an ungreased dish. Top each with one tablespoon tomato soup. Orchestrate six sausage cuts on every biscuit half, sprinkle with one tablespoon cheddar prepare for 8-10 minutes or until cheddar softens. Warmth stove to 425. Oil a pie plate. Sprinkle onion and Parmesan cheddar in pie plate. Beat milk, eggs, and bisques 15 seconds in blender on high. Fill pie plate. Heat 20 minutes. Spread pizza sauce over the top. Top with unusual ingredients. Heat 10-15 minutes, until cheddar is light darker. Cool 15 minutes.

SINGULAR PESTO PIZZAS WITH MUSHROOMS AND OLIVES RECIPE:

Ingredients:

* 1/4 cup arranged pesto
* 8 Baked Individual Pizza Crusts
* 8 substantial Spinach leaves, cut
* 1/2 cup pizza sauce
* 1/2 cup Nonfat mozzarella cheddar,
* 6 little Mushrooms, daintily cut
* 5 Black olives, daintily cut
* 1 tablespoon Parmesan cheddar, crisply ground Directions:

Preheat the stove to 400F. Splash 1/2 tablespoon of the pesto on every one of the pizza coverings. Lay a spinach leaf on top and spread with one tablespoon of the pizza sauce. Over the sauce, dissipate one tablespoon of mozzarella cheddar, at that point equivalent measures of the cut mushrooms and olives. Finish with a light sprinkling of the Parmesan cheddar. Spot the pizzas on a treat sheet and heat for 10 minutes.

CHILD-SIZED PIZZAS RECIPE

Ingredients:

*   4 English biscuits, split
*   3/4 cup pizza sauce
*   1/4-pound Canadian Bacon;
*   6 enormous mushrooms, cut
*   4 enormous dark olives, cut
*   1 little onion, cut
*   1/2 medium green pepper, cut
*   1/4-pound mozzarella cheddar,
*   1/3 cup parmesan cheddar, ground

Method:

On every biscuit, half spread two tablespoons pizza sauce. Top each with one-eighth of the Canadian bacon, mushrooms, olives, onion, and green pepper. Sprinkle each with mozzarella and parmesan cheddar, partitioning similarly. Spot on non-stick heating sheet. Heat at 350F for 10 to 15 minutes or until cheddar melts and starts to dark-colored. Serve hot.

CHILD-SIZED SOUTHWEST PIZZA RECIPE:

Ingredients:

* 6 pita bread adjusts
* 16 ounces can refry beans
* 4 ounces slashed green chilies depleted
* 1/2 cup diced tomato
* 3/4 cup cheddar
* 1 1/2 cup ice shelf lettuce
* 6 tablespoons harsh cream

Method:

Preheat grill to 400F degrees. Spot pita adjusts on a massive lobed heating sheet. Heat 8 minutes or until fresh, turning following 4 minutes. Let cool marginally. Join beans and chilies blending great. Spread around 1/3 cup bean blend over every pita round. Separation tomato equally among pizzas. Sprinkle with cheddar. Prepare 8 minutes longer or until the blend is hot and cheddar softens. Expel from the stove. Top every pizza with 1/4 cup lettuce and one tablespoon sharp cream.

LEEK TOMATO GOAT CHEESE PIZZA RECIPE

Ingredients:

* 1 1/2 tablespoon Butter
* 2 medications. leeks, daintily cut
* 1 tablespoon new parsley, minced
* 3/4 cup tomato, hacked
* 3 ounces Montrachet or Feta
* 2 tablespoons olive oil

Method:

Dissolve spread in a large skillet over medium-low warmth. Include leeks; sauté until delicate, around 10 minutes. Season with salt and pepper. Mix in parsley. Cool. Spread leek besting equitably over pizza shell; sprinkle tomatoes over. Top with cheddar. Shower 1 tablespoon oil over. Prepare around 10 minutes at 450 F. Expel from grill and brush covering with olive oil.

MINIMAL ENGLISH MUFFIN PIZZAS RECIPE:

Ingredients:

* 4 English Muffins
* 1 bundle cut pepperoni
* 1 bundle Mozzarella Cheese
* 1 container Pizza Quick Sauce

Bearings:

Split English Muffins. Toast daintily to dark-colored. Spread every half with the Pizza Quick Sauce. Spot Pepperoni on every biscuit. Top with heaps of Mozzarella Cheese. Heat 350 in broiler until the cheddar is dissolved and bubbly.

* 1/2-pound ground meat
* 1/2-pound hotdog
* 1/2-pound bacon
* 2 (8 oz) bundles of cheddar (mozzarella, pizza cheddar, and so on)
* 1 bundle of pepperoni
* 1 cup of pizza sauce

Dark-colored the ground meat with the hotdog. Channel. Blend in 1 bundle of cheddar. Spread on the base of a treat sheet. Pour the sauce over the "hull." Top the sauce with 1/2 of the 2ND bundle of cheddar. Cook the bacon; deplete and disintegrate. Include the bacon and pepperoni. Include more cheddar. Cook at

350 until darker (30 minutes roughly).

MAKE-AHEAD FRENCH BREAD PIZZA RECIPE:

Ingredients:

* 1 portion French bread
* 3 cups Spaghetti Sauce
* 1/4 cup Parmesan cheddar
* 1 cup mozzarella cheddar
* 3 ounces pepperoni cuts

Headings:

This formula is collected the day it's served. Put sauce in a 3-cup compartment, cheeses in 2-1-quart sacks, pepperoni in the 1-quart pack, envelop bread by overwhelming foil. Freeze. To Serve: Thaw French bread, sauce, ground cheeses, and pepperoni. Cut the portion of French bread down the middle the long way. Layer sauce. Parmesan cheddar, pepperoni, and mozzarella cheddar on every half. Set stove to sear and additionally 550 degrees F. Spot bread on the heating sheet, and put in the stove. Sear until mozzarella is liquefied. Cut into serving-size pieces.

Preheat grill to 500F. (Note: If the pita is genuinely tough, place amassed pizzas straightforwardly on a rack. If not, preheat a preparing sheet with the appliance.)

In a large sauté skillet, preheat oil and container over medium fire. Include onions and peppers and sweet for around five minutes to relax. Include ground meat and more oil if famous for forestalling staying. As meat tans, say a final farewell to a wooden spoon to join with veg and darker equitably. When the meat is generally separated and as yet cooking, including cumin, coriander, oregano, and a solid scramble of salt and pepper. Keep on saluting for 1-2 minutes to draw out the fragrances in the flavoring.

Include tomato glue and a sprinkle of water if the blend is dry (this will frequently rely upon how lean your meat is), diminish warmth to medium-low, and stew for 3-4 minutes to get done with cooking. In the interim, you ought to have prepared the garnishes. To amass the pizzas, start by sprinkling each with a tablespoon of Parmesan, this will assist the garnishes with sticking in the stove. Equitably isolate meat blend among the four pies. Top with feta, hacked tomato, and olives. Spot in the stove for around 10 minutes until cheddar has marginally dissolved, and the bread has gotten adequately darker and fresh. To serve, shower with olive oil and a sprinkling of some hand-torn crisp basil.

MEXICAN SALMON PIZZA RECIPE.

Ingredients:

*   Nonstock cooking splash

*   2 little bought prepared pizza hulls (around seven creeps in the distance across)

*   1/2 cup packaged salsa or Picante sauce

*   1/2 cup coarsely squashed tostadas

*   1/2 cup cooked, chopped salmon

*   1/4 cup cleaved red onion (discretionary)

*   1 cup Mexican prepared cheese** or Monterey Jack cheddar

Directions:

A bundled mix of Cheddar, Colby, and Monterey Jack cheeses with Mexican seasonings. Warmth stove to 450°F. Splash top surface of every pizza hull with non-stick shower and spot on a preparing sheet. A spread portion of salsa on each hull. Top each covering with squashed tostadas, salmon, onions, and cheddar. Prepare until cheddar is bubbly and daintily seared, 8-10 minutes.

MICROWAVE MINI PIZZAS RECIPE:

Ingredients:

* 1 (6 tallies) pkg. English biscuits
* 1 little container pizza sauce (any flavor)
* 8 ounces pkg. Mozzarella cheddar
* 48 cuts pepperoni (discretionary)

Bearings:

Pour sauce onto open-face biscuits. Spot 4 cuts of pepperoni on every biscuit. Top every biscuit with a liberal measure of cheddar. Prepare in the microwave for 2 minutes or until the cheddar is dissolved.

* 1 1/2 cup warm water (110F)
* 1 1/2 tablespoon dynamic dry yeast
* 3/4 teaspoon salt
* 1 tablespoon olive oil
* 4 cups flour
* tomato glue
* grated mozzarella cheddar
* sliced pepperoni
* ham
* salami
* onions

* pineapple
* mushrooms
* whatever

Break up yeast in warm water and let stand 5 minutes. Include the remainder of ingredients and blend well. Work for 7-8 minutes and spot in a lubed bowl. Let ascend for 1/2 hours. At the point when prepared, shape into smaller than usual pizzas (around 4-5-inch round). Stop on the treated sheet. At the point when prepared to serve, remove from more relaxed and spot on a heating sheet that has been daintily oiled and sprinkled with cornmeal. Let defrost.

Garnishes:

Sprinkle a little mozzarella on every pizza, the speed with tomato glue, include whatever garnishes and top with mozzarella. Prepare at 400F for 15-20 minutes.

MUSHROOM TURKEY AND SWISS CHEESE PIZZA RECIPE:

Ingredients:

* 4 White mushrooms
* 2 teaspoons Olive oil
* 1 little disc of Pizza (6" round)
* 3 cuts Turkey or ham (slim cuts)
* 1 medium Tomato, daintily cut
* Coarsely ground dark pepper to taste
* 2 teaspoons Chopped parsley or basil
* 3 cuts Swiss cheddar (slim cuts)

Method:

If you like a Southwestern taste to your pizza, substitute cuts of smoked chicken bosom and Monterey Jack cheddar, at that point, sprinkle with cleaved cilantro. Or then again, make an incredible Italian taste with prosciutto and mozzarella. Preheat stove to 450F. Wipe mushrooms perfect and trim stems; cut. Warmth oil in a little skillet. Include mushroom cuts and cook over high warmth for 2 minutes, shaking skillet.

PARSLEY PESTO AND FETA PHYLLO PIZZA RECIPE:

Ingredients:

* 3 cups new parsley leaves - washed and dried
* 2 cloves garlic cloves - hacked
* 1/3 cup parmesan cheddar
* 1/3 cup pine nuts - toasted until brilliant and cooled
* 1/3 cup olive oil
* 9 tablespoons parmesan cheddar - crisply ground
* 3/4 cup disintegrated feta cheddar

Method:

Preheat the stove to 400°F. Make pesto: In a nourishment processor, mix well all pesto ingredients. Pesto might be made three days ahead and chilled, surface secured with cling wrap. Softly brush a massive preparing sheet with some spread and put one sheet phyllo on margarine. Softly brush phyllo with some remaining margarine and sprinkle with one tablespoon Parmesan.

Put another sheet phyllo over cheddar, squeezing solidly with the goal that it clings to the base layer. Spread, sprinkle with cheddar, and layer remaining phyllo, in the same way, finishing with a sheet of phyllo. Gently brush the top sheet with the residual spread. Overlap in all sides 1/4 inch, squeezing to top sheet, and crease up a 1/4-inch fringe, pleating corners. Spread pesto and phyllo outside layer and sprinkle with feta. Heat pizza in the center of the grill until the covering is brilliant, around 15 minutes.

PEKING DUCK PIZZA RECIPE:

Ingredients:

* 1-pound boneless duck bosom - with skin
* 2 tablespoons hoisin sauce
* 1 cup olive oil - for browning
* 2 pizza layers (9-inch size)
* cornmeal (to tidy skillet)
* 1/4 cup hoisin sauce
* 1 1/2 cup mozzarella cheddar
* 8 scallions - white part just
* 2 cups mushrooms

Method:

Prepare duck, which has been covered with hoisin sauce and chill. Cut into 1/8-inch cuts. Fry won ton strips in hot olive oil (375 degrees) until dark-colored and fresh. Channel and put in a safe spot. Sauté mushrooms in a single tablespoon olive oil and put in a safe spot. Make or use bought pizza batter (two 9 inch adjusts). Spread 1 to 2 teaspoons of hoisin sauce over the mixture. Spread with the mozzarella, fragmented green onions, and cut duck. Spread the sautéed mushrooms over the duck. Heat (ideally on a pizza stone) at 500 degrees for 9 to 10 minutes or until cheddar is bubbly. Cut the pizza and afterward top with the won tons and shower on more hoisin sauce in a bug catching network design. Spot a pizza stone or modified preparing sheet on the most reduced broiler rack preheats stove to 500°F or most high setting. Coat a 12 1/2-INCH pizza container with cooking splash and residue with cornmeal. Cook frankfurter in a little non-stick skillet over medium warmth, abandoning time to time, until sautéed and cooked through, 10 to 12 minutes. Channel and cut into 1/4-inch-thick cuts.

In the meantime, get ready peperomia: Heat 2 teaspoons oil in a large non-stick skillet over medium warmth. Include onion and ringer pepper; cook, frequently mixing, until mellowed, 4 to 6 minutes. Include garlic and squashed red pepper; cook, mixing, for one moment. Include tomato and cook for 3 minutes. Expel from the warmth and mix in vinegar, salt, and pepper. Move to a plate and let cool. On a gently floured surface, fold the mixture into a 13-inch circle.

Move to the readied skillet. Turn edges under to make a slight edge. Brush the edge with the staying one teaspoon oil. Sprinkle mozzarella over the outside layer, leaving a 1/2-INCH outskirt. Top with the peperomia and hotdog. Sprinkle with Parmesan. Spot the pizza dish on the warmed pizza stone (or heating sheet) and prepare the pizza until the base is crisp and brilliant, 10 to 14 minutes. Serve right away.

PHILLY CHEESE STEAK CRESCENT PIZZA RECIPE:

Ingredients:

* 1 can (8-oz. size) refrigerated bow rolls
* 8 ounces meagrely cut cooked shop broil meat
* 1 tablespoon bought Italian serving of mixed greens dressing
* 1 1/2 cup mozzarella cheddar
* 2 tablespoons olive or vegetable oil
* 1 cup coarsely slashed green chime pepper
* 1 cup coarsely slashed onions
* 1/2 teaspoon hamburger season moment bouillon

Method:

Warmth grill to 375 F. Unroll batter in the ungreased 13x9-inch container. Press over the base and 1/2-inch upsides. Immovably press holes to seal. Wrap meat firmly in foil. Spot sickle batter and hamburger in a stove. Prepare at 375 F. for 10 minutes or until an outside layer is light brilliant dark-colored. Mastermind warm hamburger over halfway prepared hull. Brush with serving of mixed greens dressing. Sprinkle with cheddar. Come back to broiler; heat an extra 8 to 10 minutes or until edges of the outside layer are brilliant dark-colored and cheddar is dissolved.

Then, heat oil in a medium skillet over medium warmth until hot. Include ringer pepper, onions, and bouillon; cook and mix 3 to 5 minutes or until delicate, blending much of the time. Spoon cooked vegetables over dissolved cheddar.

PITA PESTO PIZZAS RECIPE:

Ingredients:

* 2 cloves garlic
* 1/2 cup softly stuffed parsley
* 4 cups torn spinach
* 1/2 cup ground parmesan
* 1 1/2 tablespoon dried entire basil
* 1 tablespoon lemon juice
* 2 (6-inch size) entire wheat pitas
* 1 cup slashed red chime pepper
* 1/2 cup part-skim mozzarella cheddar

Method:

Position blade sharp edge in the processor. Drop garlic and parsley through Food chute with processor running; process 15 seconds or until minced. Include spinach, parmesan, basil, and lemon juice; process 30 seconds. Scratch bowl with a flexible spatula and procedure an extra 30 seconds or until smooth. Split pita bread into four rounds, spread 2 Tbsp. Spinach Mixture over inside of every pita round. Top with chime pepper and Cheese. Heat at 450 for 5 min. Or, on the other hand, until cheddar liquefies. Serve warm.

* 1-ounce low-fat mozzarella cheddar -
* 1 pita bread
* sun-dried tomato parts - rehydrated with water and slashed
* 1 marinated artichoke heart - flushed and depleted

- * chopped or cut crisp basil
- * red pepper - hot or mellow, crisp or cooked Directions:

Shred low-fat mozzarella onto pita round, include sun-dried tomatoes, marinated artichoke heart, clips of new basil and a packaged red pepper or, daintily cut a fresh red pepper. Cook until hot and bubbly.

- * 3 ounces lean ground hamburger
- * 2 tablespoons slashed green pepper
- * 2 tablespoons canned slashed mushrooms
- * 2 tablespoons pizza sauce
- * 1/8 teaspoon dried oregano, squashed
- * 1 enormous pita bread round, split on a level plane
- * Crushed red pepper (discretionary)
- * 1 tablespoon mozzarella cheddar Directions:

In a little skillet, cook the ground hamburger and green pepper till meat is dark-colored, and green pepper is delicate. Channel off fat. Mix mushrooms, pizza sauce, and oregano into the skillet. Cook and mix around one moment or till the meat blend are warmed through. Spread meat blend more than one pita bread half. (Store remaining pita bread half for another utilization.) Sprinkle with squashed red pepper, whenever wanted. Top with cheddar. Spot pita bread on a heating sheet. Sear 3 to 4 creeps from the heat around 2 minutes or till cheddar dissolves.

For outside layer, evidence yeast with support in warm water. Blend yeast, water, and olive oil mix in flour 1 cup at once. Turn out onto the floured surface, massage until smooth, 5 to 7 moments, including flour as fundamental. The batter will be delicate. A spot in an oiled bowl, going to cover all sides, spread with cling wrap and let ascend in a warm spot until multiplied. Punch down and let rest 15 mins. Separation down the middle a press out into two 12-inch round pizza containers or 10x15x1 dish or 1 of each. Sprinkled with yellow cornmeal (prevents outside layer from staying). For the sauce, finely hack tomatoes in can with a blade, saving juice. Warmth olive oil in a medium pot over medium warmth. Include onion, cook 5 minutes, or until delicate. Include garlic, cook 30 sec. More Add tomatoes with fluid, tomato glue, oregano, basil, 1/2-teaspoon sugar, 1/2-TEASPOON salt, and dark pepper. Bring to a bubble over high warmth. Diminish warmth to medium-low. Stew, revealed 10-15 minutes until thickened. Mixing incidentally.

Substitute layers in the simmering pot as follows: cheeseburger, noodles, cheddar, soup, mushrooms and olives, onions, sauce, and pepperoni. Warmth on low in simmering pot for 4 hours.

PIZZA ARIZONA RECIPE:

Ingredients:

* 2 teaspoons yellow cornmeal
* 1 (10-OUNCE) tube refrigerated pizza batter
* 1 1/2 cup bought chipotle salsa
* 2 tablespoons olive oil
* 1 1/2 teaspoon stew powder
* 1 1/2 cup Mexican-style four-cheddar blend or pizza cheddar
* 1/4 cup hacked crisp cilantro

Method:

Position rack in base third of stove and preheat to 400 F. Sprinkle cornmeal on heating sheet. Unroll mixture onto the sheet, framing 10X15-INCH square shape. Blend salsa, oil, and stew powder in a little bowl. Hurl cheddar and cilantro in a medium bowl. Spoon salsa blend over mixture, leaving 1/2-INCH outskirt. Sprinkle with cheddar blend. Prepare pizza until the hull is brilliant, dark-colored, and cheddar is liquefied and rising, around 15 minutes. Cut into squares and serve.

PIZZA FOR EASY BAKE OVEN RECIPE:

Ingredients:
* 2 tablespoons All-reason flour
* 1/8 teaspoon Baking powder
* 1 run Salt
* 1 teaspoon Margarine
* 2 1/4 teaspoons Milk
* 1 tablespoon Pizza sauce
* 1 1/2 tablespoon Shredded mozzarella cheddar

Method:

Mix flour, preparing powder, salt, and margarine until the mixture seems as though medium-sized pieces. Gradually include milk while mixing. Shape mixture into a ball and spot into a lobed dish. Utilize your fingers to pat the mixture uniformly over the base of the skillet, at that point up the sides. Pour the sauce equitably over the batter, at that point, sprinkle with the cheddar. Heat 20 mins. Expel.

* 1 1/3 cup warm water (105F)
* 1/4 cup Non-fat dry milk
* 1/2 teaspoon salt
* 4 cups Flour
* 1 tablespoon Sugar
* 1 pk. Dry yeast
* 2 tablespoons Vegetable oil (for batter)

* 9 ounces Vegetable oil (3 oz. per dish)
* Butter seasoned Pam

Sauce

* 1 (8 Ounce) Can Tomato Sauce
* 1 teaspoon Dry Oregano
* 1/2 teaspoon Marjoram
* 1/2 teaspoon Dry Basil
* 1/2 teaspoon Garlic salt

Put yeast, sugar, salt, and dry milk in a large (2 qt.) bowl. Add water and mix to blend well. Permit to sit for two minutes. Include oil and mix once more. Include flour and mix until batter structures and flour is assimilated. Turn out onto a level surface and ply for around 10 minutes. Partition mixture into three balls. In three 9" cake skillet, put 3 Oz. of oil in each ensuring it is spread uniformly. Utilizing a moving pin, reveal every mixture ball to around a 9" circle. A spot in cake container. Splash the external edge of the mixture with Pam. Spread with a plate. Spot in the warm region and permit to ascend for 1 to 1/2 hours. Join ingredients and let sit for 60 minutes.

For Each Nine Inch Pizza: 1. Preheat stove to 475F 2. Spoon 1/3 cup sauce on the mixture and spread to inside 1" of edge. 3. Convey 1/2 Oz. mozzarella cheddar on the sauce. 4. Spot garnishes of your decision in a specific order: Pepperoni or Ham Vegetables Meats (cooked ground hotdog or hamburger) 5. Top with 3 Oz. Mozzarella cheddar 6. Cook until cheddar is foaming, and the external outside layer is dark-colored.

PIZZA PESTO VERDE RECIPE.

Ingredients:

* 1 (12-or 14-inch size) pizza covering
* 2 cups mozzarella,
* 1 cup feta,
* 1 cup arranged pesto sauce
* 1 cup spinach, cleaved
* 1 cup canned tomatoes, diced

Method:

Preheat stove to 425 degrees F. Spread pesto sauce on somewhat heated covering and top with slashed spinach. Sprinkle mozzarella equitably over the sauce, at that point top with tomatoes and feta. Prepare around 15 minutes or until the mozzarella is softened, and the covering is fresh and brilliant.

Chicken Pesto: For a heartier adaptation, supplant the spinach with 1 cup cooked chicken (or cubed). Proceed with cheeses and tomatoes. Chicken Mushroom Pesto: Mushrooms make it significantly heartier. Supplant the spinach with 1 cup cooked chicken (or cubed) and 1 cup canned mushrooms (cut and depleted). Proceed with cheeses and tomatoes. Spot rice cakes on the prepared sheet. Spread pizza Sauce equally on each rice cake; top with unusual ingredients. Prepare at 400F degrees for 10 minutes.

PIZZA RUSTIC RECIPE:

Ingredients:

* 1 portion solidified or new bread mixture
* 1/3 cup ground parmesan cheddar
* 1 clove garlic, hacked
* 1 tablespoon olive oil
* 1 bundle (9oz size) hacked crisp spinach
* 2 medium tomatoes; peeled, seeded, and hacked
* 1 tablespoon basil
* 1/8 teaspoon sage
* 4 ounces provolone
* 4 ounces daintily cut Prosciutto
* 1 cup mozzarella
* 1 egg white
* 1 tablespoon water

Method:

Allow batter to rise; when done, work parmesan into the mixture. In a medium skillet, sauté garlic in olive oil for 30 seconds. Include spinach mix one moment, sauté just until spinach shrinks, include savvy, put in a safe spot.

Mix tomato and basil put in a safe spot. Pat 1/2 the batter into a pie container and layer (in a specific order) the accompanying ingredients, leaving a 1-inch fringe: 1 cup of the mozzarella, sautéed spinach, all the provolone, tomato and basil blend, the meat, and the rest of the mozzarella. Turn out the outstanding mixture and spot it on the pie and seal edges together. Put in a safe spot and let ascend for 60 minutes. Preheat stove to 375F. Brush egg and water blend on top. Heat for 40 minutes or until pie turns somewhat dark-colored. You may need to put aluminum foil over the pie throughout the previous 10 minutes to forestall overcooking.

PIZZA SANTA FE STYLE RECIPE:

Ingredients:

* 1 (12-inch) pizza outside, prepared to heat
* 1 1/2 cup daintily stuffed cilantro leaves
* 1/2 cup daintily stuffed parsley leaves
* 2 cloves garlic
* 1 jalapeno chile, split, seeded
* 1 scallion, cut in pieces
* 1 tablespoon lemon juice
* 1/2 cup olive oil
* salt and newly ground pepper to taste
* 2 Anaheim or gentle green chiles, broiled, peeled, seedles, cut into strips
* 5 tomatillos (or substitute green tomatoes), husked, washed, cut
* 4 little tomatoes, cut and dried on paper towels
* 1 little red onion, daintily cut
* salt and newly ground pepper
* 1 tablespoon cleaved crisp oregano or 1/2 teaspoon dried
* 2 cups ground jack cheddar

Method:

Join all sauce ingredients aside from salt and pepper in a nourishment processor or blender. Puree until smooth. Add salt and pepper to taste. Preheat stove to 450 F. Spot pizza outside on an enormous heating sheet. Channel and cut artichoke hearts. Preheat grill to 450F. On softly oiled preparing sheet, press chilled mixture into 9 x 12-inch square shape; pleat edges to frame an edge. Brush with a large portion of the oil. Equitably sprinkle with wheat or cornmeal; press gently into the batter. Sprinkle with garlic. Mastermind onion in 1 layer over batter; top with artichoke hearts. Sprinkle with residual oil. Softly season with salt and pepper. Equitably sprinkle with cheddar. Try not to allow the batter to rise. The pizza might be held quickly in the fridge before heating. Prepare 15 minutes or until the outside layer is brilliant darker.

PIZZA WITH PORK AND PEPPERS RECIPE:

Ingredients:

* 1/2 teaspoon oregano
* 1/2 teaspoon salt
* 1/2 teaspoon garlic powder
* 1/8 teaspoon pepper
* 1 (1-POund) pork tenderloin, cut in 1/4-BY-3-INCH strips
* 1 cup meagrely cut onion
* 1 tablespoon olive oil
* 1 red ringer pepper, cut in flimsy strips
* 1 green ringer pepper, cut in flimsy strips
* 1 Boboli pizza outside layer
* 1 cup packaged tomato pasta sauce
* 1 cup diminished fat mozzarella

Method:

Preheat grill to 450 degrees. Join the oregano, salt, garlic powder, and pepper in a bowl. Include pork strips and hurl until the seasonings hold fast to the meat. Include the onions and hurl. Warmth the oil in a large non-stick skillet. Include the pork and onions and cook, blending, 3 to 4 minutes, until the onions are somewhat relaxed. Add the peppers to the skillet and cook, blending much of the time, another 3 to 4 minutes, or until the pork is scarcely pink. Spot the pizza hull on a treat sheet. Spread the tomato sauce over the outside layer, leaving a 1-inch outskirt around the edges. Spot the cooked pork and peppers over the sauce and top with the cheddar. Prepare for 10 minutes, or until the cheddar is softened and the hull warmed through.

Spot a pizza stone or rearranged heating sheet on the most minimal stove rack preheat grill to 500°F or most high setting. Coat a 12 1/2-INCH pizza container with cooking splash and residue with cornmeal. Join beans, one tablespoon oil, rosemary, garlic, and squashed red pepper in a medium bowl; hurl to cover. On a gently floured surface, fold the batter into a 13-INCH circle. Move to the readied skillet. Turn edges under to make a slight edge. Brush the edge with the staying one teaspoon oil.

Spread sauce over the outside, leaving a 1/2-inch fringe. Sprinkle with 1/4 cup Parmesan. Spread the bean blend on top. Sprinkle with prosciutto and onion. Top with the staying 1/4 cup Parmesan. Crush pepper over the top. Spot the pizza container on the warmed pizza stone (or heating sheet) and prepare the pizza until the base is fresh and brilliant, 10 to 14 minutes. Dissipate arugula over the pizza and serve right away.

POLENTA PIZZERIA RECIPE:

Ingredients:

* 2 quarts water
* 2 cups polenta
* 16 ounces soy mozzarella cheddar
* 1/2 teaspoon dried bean stew pepper drops
* 1/2 cup vegan pizza sauce
* 2 enormous, not too mature, washed
* 1 enormous green pepper, washed and deseeded
* 12 ounces box mushrooms, cleaned off

Method:

Preheat grill to 350F. Put water in a large pot or Dutch stove and heat to the point of boiling over high warmth. In the interim mesh, the soy cheddar and put in a safe spot. At the point when water is bubbling, gradually pour in the polenta while mixing simultaneously. Decrease warmth to medium-low and keep mixing the polenta at regular intervals to maintain a strategic distance from knots and forestall scorching. You may need to cover the pot with a top somewhat as the polenta will, in general, beginning spitting as it thickens.

It should take around 20 minutes for the polenta to become as thick as porridge. Meanwhile, finely cleave the green pepper and cut the mushrooms and tomatoes. Warmth some nonfat cooking splash in a skillet, include peppers and mushrooms and sauté a couple of moments over medium warmth until the juices have been discharged. Channel off overabundance juice. At the point when the polenta has thickened, turn off the warmth and mix in half of the ground soy mozzarella and the entirety of the dried pepper chips. Move the polenta to a 10" by 15" rectangular glass or tempered steel broiler dish and spread out uniformly. Let cool for 15 minutes while you enjoy a reprieve. At the point when the polenta has adequately cooled, spread the pizza sauce equitably ridiculous, trailed by the tomato cuts, green peppers, and mushrooms. Sprinkle rest of the soy mozzarella on the vegetables, trailed by the Italian flavoring. Spot dish in the broiler on lower rack and prepare 15-20 minutes until warmed through and cheddar has liquefied.

SPRING UP PIZZA CASSEROLE RECIPE:

Ingredients:

* 1 1/2-pound Hamburger
* 1 cup Onion; slashed
* 1 cup Green pepper; slashed
* 1 clove Garlic
* 1/2 teaspoon Oregano
* 1 run Salt
* 1/2 cup Water
* 1/8 teaspoon Hot pepper sauce
* 1 bundle Spaghetti sauce blend (1.5OZ)
* 1 cup Milk
* 1 cup Flour
* 1 tablespoon Oil
* 2 Eggs
* 1/2 teaspoon salt
* 7 ounces Monterey Jack or Mozzarella cheddar cuts
* 1/2 cup Parmesan cheddar; ground

Method:

Preheat grill to 400 f. In a considerable skillet, dark-colored burger, and channel. Mix in onion, green pepper, garlic, oregano, salt, water, hot pepper sauce, tomato sauce, and sauce blend; stew around 10 min was mixing periodically. In a bowl, consolidate milk, oil, and eggs; beat 1 min on medium speed. Include flour and salt; beat 2 min or until smooth. Empty hot meat blend into 13X9 container; top with cheddar cuts. Pour hitter over cheddar, covering filling totally; sprinkle with Parmesan cheddar. Heat at 400 f for 25-30 min or until puffed and brilliant.

POTATO PIZZA BAKE RECIPE:

Ingredients:

* 1-pound ground hamburger
* 4 cups meagrely cut potatoes
* 1 drug. onion (cut slender)
* one would cheddar be able to cheddar soup
* 1 soup can drain
* 1 (15 oz.) would tomato be able to sauce
* Salt and pepper to taste
* 1/2 teaspoon oregano
* 1/2 teaspoon sugar
* 1 tablespoon margarine
* 6 ounces cut mozzarella cheddar

Method:

Preheat grill to 375 F. Cook ground meat in skillet until it loses redness. Spot potatoes and onions in buttered 9x13" container. Add meat to blend. Blend cheddar soup and milk until smooth and add to basics; combine. Join tomato sauce, salt, pepper, oregano, and sugar. Pour sauce over the top, however, doesn't blend. Speck with the spread. Spread dish with foil. Prepare at 375 F for 60 minutes. Expel cover and mastermind cut cheddar on top. Sprinkle with Parmesan. Come back to the grill, revealed, for around 15 minutes or until cheddar bubbles.

PROSCIUTTO TOMATO PIZZA RECIPE

Ingredients:

* one would tomato be able to sauce; (8-ounce size)
* 1 teaspoon Italian flavoring
* 1 clove Garlic; finely hacked
* 3 cups Shredded mozzarella or Fontina Cheese
* 1 little Onion; daintily cut and Separated into rings
* 1/4 cup Grated Parmesan cheddar
* 2 tablespoons Chopped new basil leaves
* 1/2-pound Prosciutto
* 2 substantial tomatoes

Outside layer

* 1 bundle Active dry yeast
* 1 cup warm water (105 to 115 degrees)
* 2 1/2 cups All-reason flour
* 2 tablespoons Olive or vegetable oil
* 1 teaspoon Sugar
* 1 teaspoon salt

Method:

Spot broiler rack in the least position. Oil 2 treat sheets or 12-INCH pizza dish. Warmth stove to 425 degrees F. Gets Ready Crust. Blend tomato sauce, Italian flavoring, and garlic. Cut prosciutto or thoroughly cooked smoked ham into julienne strips (2 X 1/4 X 1/8 inch). Partition batter down the middle. Pat every half into 11-INCH hover on treat sheet with floured fingers. Top with tomato sauce blend, onion, and Fontina cheddar. Sprinkle with basil, prosciutto, and plum tomatoes (coarsely cleaved). Top with Parmesan cheddar. Prepare each pizza in turn 15 to 20 minutes or until outside is brilliant dark-colored.

PUMPKIN PIZZAS RECIPE:

Ingredients:

* 4 (6-inch) Italian bread shells
* 2/3 cup pizza or spaghetti sauce
* 1 bundle (3-1/2 ounces) pepperoni cuts
* 4 cuts (1 ounce every) American cheddar, cut into triangles
* 1/4 cup broccoli florets
* 2 cherry tomatoes, split

Method:

Preheat stove to 375F. Spot bread shells on ungreased preparing sheets. Spread pizza sauce equitably on bread shells; top equally with pepperoni cuts. Spot cheddar triangles on pizza sauce to make jack-o'- lamp faces. Include broccoli florets for eyes and tomatoes, split, for noses. Heat 10 to 12 minutes or until cheddar is softened.

REUBEN PIZZA RECIPE

Ingredients:

* 1 portion (16-ounce size) solidified entire wheat bread mixture, defrosted

* 1/2 cup Thousand Island serving of mixed greens dressing

* 2 cups Swiss cheddar

* 6 ounces meagrely cut cooked corned hamburger

* 1 can (8-ounce size) sauerkraut, flushed and very much depleted

* 1/2 teaspoon caraway seed

* Dill pickle cuts, slashed (discretionary)

Method:

Preheat grill to 375 degrees F. On a softly floured surface, fold bread mixture into a 14-INCH circle. Move to a lobed 13-INCH pizza container. Develop edges marginally. Prick liberally with a fork. Heat for 20 to 25 minutes or until light darker. A spread portion of the serving of mixed greens dressing over hot outside layer. Sprinkle with half of the Swiss cheddar. Organize corned hamburger over cheddar. Shower remaining serving of mixed greens dressing over corned meat. Top with sauerkraut and staying Swiss cheddar. Sprinkle with caraway seed. Prepare around 10 minutes more or until cheddar melts and pizza is warmed through. Top with hacked dill pickle, whenever wanted. Preheat stove to 450 degrees F. Softly oil a massive preparing sheet. In a considerable bowl, combine rice, eggs, and mozzarella. Press into the heating sheet to frame a thick hull. Prepare outside layer until delicately caramelized (15 to 20 minutes). In a large bowl, join pizza sauce, oregano, basil, and garlic. Spoon over prepared hull. Top with Parmesan, artichoke hearts, and olives. Prepare ten additional minutes, at that point, cut, and serve.

FIRM SWEET ONION PIZZA RECIPE:

Ingredients:

* 1 (12-inch) prebaked pizza shell
* 2 1/2 tablespoons olive oil
* 1-pound sweet onions split, cut vertically
* 1/4 cup sun-dried tomatoes (stuffed in oil), slashed
* 1/2 teaspoon dried oregano
* 1/2 teaspoon dried thyme
* 1/2 teaspoon dried basil
* Salt and pepper to taste

Method:

Warmth stove to 425 degrees. Spot pizza shell on heating sheet; sprinkle onions on pizza and shower with olive oil; top with sun-dried tomatoes. Sprinkle with herbs, salt, and pepper. Heat until onions simply start to dark-colored, around 10 minutes.

Preheat grill to 450 degrees F. Shower a 12-inch pizza dish with vegetable cooking splash. Fold or stretch batter into skillet framing a 1/4-inch edge around the edge. Utilizing a fork, puncture surface of the batter. Prepare until outside is brilliant, 10 to 12 minutes; put in a safe spot. Then, in a large skillet over medium-high warmth, heat olive oil until it just starts to smoke. Include mushrooms, onion, and garlic; cook, mixing at times, until mushrooms are brilliant, around 5 minutes. Include balsamic vinegar, thyme, salt, and dark pepper; cook and mix until the fluid has about dissipated, 1 to 2 minutes; put in a safe spot. Spread pesto over held pizza outside layer; sprinkle with 1/2 cup of the cheddar. Top with saved mushrooms blend and broiled peppers; sprinkle with staying 1/2 cup cheddar. Prepare until hot and cheddar is softened, around 10 minutes. Cut in wedges; serve right away.

EXCITING SALMON PIZZA RECIPE:

Ingredients:

* Nonstock cooking splash

* 2 little bought prepared pizza hulls (every seven crawls in the distance across)

* 1/2 cup pizza sauce

* 1/2 cup cooked, chopped salmon

* 1/4 cup cleaved red onion (discretionary)

* 1 cup mozzarella cheddar

Method:

Warmth stove to 450°F. Splash top surface of every pizza outside layer with non-stick shower. A spread portion of the pizza sauce on each outside. Top with salmon, onion, and afterward cheddar. Heat until cheddar is bubbly and delicately seared, 8-10 minutes.
Preheat the grill to 230 C/450 F. Combine the garlic, tomatoes, tomato glue, olive oil, salt, and pepper. Spread a far layer equitably over the pizza outside. Orchestrate the basil, green pepper, and fish uniformly over the pizza covering. Spot the cubed cheddar equally on top. Spot the pizza straightforwardly on the broiler rack and cook for 12 minutes. Slice into six cuts to serve.

MESSY JOE PIZZA RECIPE:

Ingredients:

* 1-pound ground hamburger
* 3/4 cup ketchup or messy joe sauce
* 1/2 cup cut green onions
* 1 teaspoon prepared salt
* 1 enormous arranged pizza outside - 12 inch
* 1 1/2 cup cheddar - your decision

Method:

Preheat grill to 425F degrees. In a large non-stick skillet, darker the ground meat over medium warmth 8 to 10 minutes or until not, at this point pink, blending sporadically. Channel. Mix in ketchup, green onions, and flavoring; heat through. Spot pizza outside layer on a massive heating sheet. Top uniformly with meat blend and sprinkle with cheddar. Heat 12 to 15 minutes or until cheddar is softened.

Warmth fire cook to 425 degrees. In a large non-stick skillet, decrease tinted ground cheeseburger over medium warmth 8 to 10 minutes or until not, by and by pink, blending by some fortuitous event. Pour off drippings. Blend in corn, barbecue sauce, green onions, and salt, at whatever point required; heat through. Spot bread shell on a large warming sheet. Top correspondingly with cheeseburger mix; sprinkle with cheddar. Warmth 12 to 15 minutes or until cheddar combines; cut into wedges.

SMOKED SALMON AND FENNEL POTATO PIZZA RECIPE:

Ingredients:

* 2 tablespoons olive oil
* 1 medium onion
* 2 cups finely cut the new fennel bulb
* Salt and regularly ground pepper, to taste
* 1/2 cup white wine
* 3 medium potatoes, peeled
* 1/2 cup minced chives or green onion
* 1 tablespoon corn-starch
* Salt and regularly ground pepper, to taste
* 2 tablespoons olive oil
* 1/2-pound smoked salmon, cut
* 2 tablespoons minced chives or green onion
* 3 tablespoons cruel cream, mixed
* Freshly ground pepper, to taste

Method:

Void oil into a hot frypan, join onions and fennel, sauté for 5 minutes. Season with salt and pepper, join wine, lower warmth, and stew for 10-15 minutes until vegetables are sensitive and liquid has disseminated. While fennel is cooking, pound potatoes onto an ideal tea towel, move towel up and press ground potatoes dry, move to a bowl. Circuit chives, corn-starch, salt, and pepper, throw well to mix.

Warmth a massive 10 to 12" (25.530 cm) frypan over medium-high warmth, join oil, by then the potato mix. Using a large spatula, press potatoes down to cover the base of holder correspondingly, hold pushing down and cook for 5-6 minutes, circumspectly flip over and continue beating and cooking for another 5-6 minutes until dispersed and sensational. Slide onto a platter, spread with the warm fennel, top with smoked salmon and chives, sprinkle with sharp cream, and finish with heaps of usually ground pepper. Serve immediately.

SMOKY SALMON PIZZA RECIPE:

Ingredients:

*   1 can (7-1/2 oozes.) salmon, exhausted and chipped
*   1 (12 inches) facilitated pizza structure or Italian bread shell
*   cooking sprinkle
*   1 pack (3 oozes.) cream cheddar, relieved
*   1/2 cup red onion, humble cut or separated green onion
*   1/2 teaspoon squashed dried red pepper chips
*   1 1/2 cup decimated smoked cheddar (Swiss, Cheddar or mozzarella)

Method:

Preheat stove to 400 degrees. Spot pizza outside layer on treat sheet spread gently with a sprinkle. Spread cream cheddar over the structure. Join salmon, vegetables, red pepper, and cheddar. Get ready 10 to 12 minutes until cheddar is mollified.

Warmth stove to 450 degrees Fahrenheit. In a large non-stick skillet, decrease disguised ground meat over medium warmth 8 to 10 minutes or until burger isn't, by and by pink, disconnecting into 3/4-inch isolates. Season with salt; oust from skillet with an opened spoon. Spot bread shell on ungreased pizza skillet or large masterminding sheet. Spread salsa over shell; sprinkle with 1/2 of cheddar. Top additionally with meat, chilies, tomatoes, red onion, and remaining cheddar.

Warmth in 450 degrees Fahrenheit over for 11 to 13 minutes or until embellish hot and cheddar is disintegrated. Sprinkle with cilantro; cut into eight wedges. Serve immediately.

SOUTHWEST BEEF AND CHILE PIZZA RECIPE:

Ingredients:

*   1-pound ground cheeseburger
*   1/4 teaspoon salt
*   1 created pizza shell (12-inch size)
*   1 1/4 cup smooth thick salsa
*   1 1/2 cup demolished Mexican cheddar blend or Monterey jack cheddar
*   4 ounces diced green chilies, drained well
*   2 medium plum tomatoes, seeded and hacked
*   1/2 irrelevant red onion, gently cut
*   2 tablespoons hacked new cilantro

Method:

Preheat the stove to 450F. In a large non-stick skillet, reduce covered the ground meat over medium warmth for 8 to 10 minutes, isolating it as it cooks. Season with the salt; channel. Recognize the pizza shell on an ungreased pizza dish. Spread the salsa over the shell by then sprinkle with 3/4 cup cheddar. Top with the cheeseburger, by then the chilies, tomatoes, onion, and the remaining 3/4 cup cheddar. Blend sauce ingredients put in a safe spot. Warmth Oven to 425 degrees Separation batter into equal parts. On gently lobed 12" pizza dish sprinkled with a light covering of corn supper, pat every 50% of batter out into a 10 to 12-inch hover on pizza container. Separation sauce equally between pizza outside layers and spread out. Sprinkle every pizza with 1/4 cup Parmesan Cheese.

Sauté' frankfurter until nearly done, blending to separate. Include the peppers, onions, mushrooms, olives, and pepperoni and keep cooking until frankfurter is done. Dump the skillet brimming with cooked garnishes in a colander to deplete. Channel well overall. Sprinkle fixings equally onto the highest points of pizzas. Sprinkle 1 cup Mozzarella Cheese on every one of the pizzas. Prepare 20 to 25 minutes on the lower rack of the stove at 425 degrees until the hull is dark-colored and filling is hot and bubbly.

Warmth for 11 to 12 minutes, or until the fixing is hot and the cheddar is broken down. Remove from the stove and sprinkle sensibly with the cilantro. Cut into wedges and serve immediately.
Warmth 2 Tbsp. Oil in a liberal medium pot over medium warmth. Circuit onions and cook until high, mixing only from time to time, around 5 minutes. Blend in tomato sauce, garlic, oregano, and Italian enhancing. Stew until thickened, around five minutes. Warmth remaining 1 Tbsp. Oil in a skillet over medium heat. Circuit mushrooms and zucchini and cook until tricky, mixing now and again, around five minutes. Put in a protected spot. Preheat grill to 350F. Spot tortillas on getting ready sheet and warmth until crisp, around 4 minutes. Spread around 1/4 cup sauce over each. Sprinkle each with 1/4 cup cheddar. Top pizzas with mushrooms, zucchini, peppers, and olives. Get ready until cheddar isolates, around 5 minutes. Serve.

SPAM PINEAPPLE PIZZA RECIPE:

Ingredients:

* 1 can Refrigerated all-readied pizza structure (10 oz)
* 1 pack Sliced Provolone cheddar (6 oz)
* 1 can SPAM Luncheon Meat, cut in humble squares (12 oz)
* 1 can Chunk pineapple, drained (8 oz)
* 1/2 cup Thinly cut red onion
* 1/2 cup Chopped green pepper

Directions:

Warmth stove to 425'F. Oil 12" pizza dish or 13x9" getting ready skillet. Unroll hitter; press in the orchestrated dish. Top with cheddar. Driving force remaining ingredients over cheddar. Warmth 25-30 minutes or until the outside is critical wonderful darker. Warmth stove to 425 degrees. In a large skillet, sauté vegetables in oil until sensitive. Spoon sautéed vegetables and cubed Spam on to pizza outside layer set on a planning sheet or pizza skillet. Spoon spaghetti sauce over Spam. Sprinkle with cheddar. Plan for 10 to 15 minutes or until cheddar is isolated and bubbly. Spot spinach in a large non-stick skillet secured with cooking shower; spread and cook over low warmth 7 minutes or until spinach contracts, mixing now and again. Fling with pepper, and put in a protected spot. Cut move into two halves the long way; place, cut sides up, on a planning sheet. Cook 2 minutes or until splendid.

Join tomato stick, Italian seasoning, and garlic; blend well and spread over the cut sides of bread. Top with spinach mix, egg, and cheddar. Cook 2 minutes or until cheddar pacifies.

STUFFED CRUST PEPPERONI PIZZA RECIPE:

Ingredients:

* 1 can (10 oz size) Pillsbury Refrigerated Pizza Crust
* 7 pieces string cheddar
* 1/2 cup Pizza Sauce
* 20 cuts Pepperoni
* 1 cup Shredded Mozzarella Cheese

Method:

Warmth stove to 425 degrees F. Oil 13 x 9 - inch compartment. Unroll hitter and press in the base and 1-inch up sides of lobed skillet. Spot bits of string cheddar along inside edges of the player. Cover the 1 inch of the blend over and around the cheddar; press hitter edges to seal. Top the covering with sauce, pepperoni, and cheddar. Get ready at 425 degrees F for 15 to 18 minutes or until the outside layer is splendid darker and cheddar is condensed. Preheat the stove to 375 degrees. Recognize a two 1/2-FOOT-Long sheet of aluminum foil on a 12-to 14-INCH pizza holder. In a large skillet, cook the sausage, mushrooms, onion, and pepper over medium-high warmth for 10 minutes, or until the frank is sautéed and the vegetables are fork-fragile, blending every so often; channel. Spot 1 pizza cheddar side up on the skillet and spread the wiener mix consistently over the pizza.

Top with the remainder of the pizza cheddar side down, crushing the pizzas together. Overlay and seal the aluminum foil over the stuffed pizza. Get ready for 20 to 25 minutes, or until warmed through. Uncover the pizza; brush the top with the oil and sprinkle consistently with the cheddar. Get ready, uncovered, for 15 to 20 minutes, or until the cheddar is splendid.

EXCEPTIONAL PIZZA RECIPE:

Ingredients:

*   1 colossal Boboli Pizza Shell
*   5 ounces Pizza Sauce
*   2 ounces Provolone cheddar
*   2 ounces Pepperoni
*   1-ounce Canadian bacon
*   1-ounce Hard salami
*   2 ounces Mozzarella
*   2 ounces Black olives
*   1 pizza outside layer
*   1/3 cup rice wine vinegar
*   3 tablespoons soy sauce
*   3 tablespoons thick, nutty spread
*   2 tablespoons lime juice
*   3 pigeons garlic - minced
*   1 tablespoon minced fresh ginger
*   1/4 teaspoon dim pepper
*   1/4 teaspoon squashed red pepper
*   1/2-pound medium shrimp - stripped
*   1 tablespoon corn-starch

* 1/3 cup water
* 1 cup pulverized mozzarella cheddar
* 1/2 cup cut red toll pepper
* 1/2 cup cut newborn child corn
* 1/4 cup cut green onions
* 2 tablespoons cut new cilantro

Method:

Plan Pizza Crust. Preheat stove to 450°F. Unite vinegar, soy sauce, nutty spread, lime juice, garlic, ginger, dull pepper, and squashed red pepper in 2-CUP glass measure; blend to join. Give colossal skillet nonstock cooking sprinkle. Warmth over medium-high warmth until hot. Incorporate shrimp; cook and blend 5 to 7 minutes or until shrimp turn pink and dull. Move shrimp to a little bowl. Add vinegar mixture to the same skillet; warmth to the point of bubbling. Reduce warmth to medium-low and stew 3 to 4 minutes or until to some degree thickened. Merge corn-starch and water in a little bowl; blend until smooth.

Add corn-starch mix to vinegar mix in skillet; cook and blend around 5 minutes or until thickened. Oust from heat. Sprinkle cheddar over blend. Spread vinegar mix consistently over cheddar. Top with shrimp, ringer pepper, fresh child corn, and green onions. Warmth 18 to 20 minutes or until the covering is splendid darker, and cheddar is condensed. Sprinkle with cilantro.

THAI PIZZA II RECIPE:

Ingredients:

* 1 Pizza Dough Shell (uncooked) Sauce
* 2/3 cup smooth nutty spread
* 3 tablespoons Hoisin Sauce
* 2 tablespoons rice vinegar
* 1 tablespoon sesame oil Toppings
* 6 ounces Monterrey Jack cheddar
* 1 cup bean develops
* 1/2-pound little shrimp, cooked, shelled, and deveined
* 1/4 cup finely sliced green onions
* crushed dried hot chilies, to taste

Method:

Preheat oven to 450F. Spread sauce somewhat over covering. Top with shrimp and onions, by then cheddar. Warmth until cheddar starts to dim hued, 12 to 15 minutes. Oust from the grill, top with bean sprouts and pepper pieces, cut and serve. Warmth, a large nonstock skillet secured with cooking sprinkle over medium-high warmth. Incorporate mushrooms; sauté 5 minutes. Remove from heat.

Solidify ricotta and Parmesan cheeses. Spot pizza outside on a warming sheet. Spread pasta sauce over the structure, leaving a 1-INCH periphery. Contact ricotta cheddar mix consistently over sauce and top with mushrooms. Sprinkle with mozzarella.

Warmth 12 minutes or until the frame is new. Sprinkle with basil; cut into wedges.

FRENCH BREAD PIZZA RECIPE:

Ingredients:

*   1/2-pound cut pepperoni
*   1 divide French bread
*   30 ounces holder spaghetti or pizza sauce
*   Sliced dim olives
*   Sliced new mushrooms
*   16 ounces mozzarella cheddar, devastated
*   **Optional Toppings**: Candied bacon, green peppers, onion, ground meat

Method:

Chop bread down the center longwise. Spot on treat sheets. Spread bread with the sauce right to the edges. Top with sausage and pepperoni; by then, with whatever fixings are needed, complete with the chopped cheddar. Warmth the bread pizzas 20 minutes at 350 degrees. Cut into pieces. To freeze, wrap unbaked pizza immovably in foil. By then, freeze. Open up and defrost the pizzas before warming.

Preheat grill to 425 degrees. Coat 2 getting ready sheets with cooking shower.

Warmth the oil in a large nonstick skillet over medium-high. Incorporate the onion and cook, blending, 3 to 4 minutes, or until the onion is loose. Incorporate the turkey and the taco enhancing mix and cook, blending to isolate the turkey into melts, for 5 to 7 minutes, or until it is caramelized. Blend in the tomatoes and cook another 5 to 6 minutes, or until the liquid has cooked down.

Meanwhile, spread a cast-iron skillet with a cooking sprinkle and cook the tortillas, one without a moment's delay, on the different sides until crisp, around 2 minutes on each side. Move the crisped tortillas to the planning sheets.

Spoon the turkey mixture over the tortillas, spreading it consistently. Sprinkle the "pizzas" with the olives and the cheddar and get ready until the cheddar is melts around 6 to 7 minutes.

TRI-STATE PIZZA RECIPE:

Ingredients:

* 6 ounces tomato no salt included
* 8 ounces tomato sauce no salt included
* 20 ounces pizza blend
* 1/4 teaspoon squashed red pepper
* 1 teaspoon Italian enhancing
* 1 clove garlic - minced fine
* 1 little onion - minced
* 8 ounces mushrooms - cut
* 8 ounces Italian six cheddar
* 5 ounces Canadian bacon - diced
* 3 ounces pepperoni cuts
* vegetable cooking shower

Method:

Warmth grill to 400 F. Mix the tomato stick, tomato sauce, squashed red pepper, Italian enhancing, onion, and garlic together in a little bowl. Shower 2 pizza dish with a vegetable sprinkle. Parcel blend into equal parts and spread similarly in every compartment. Segment the sauce even-handedly between the two-skillet spreading consistently over the hitter. Top each pizza with the pepperoni, Canadian bacon, and mushrooms. Sprinkle with the cheddar. Warmth at 400 F for 18 minutes.

TRUFFLE PIZZA RECIPE:

Ingredients:

* 1 tablespoon Yeast
* 1 cup warm water (110 degrees)
* 1/4 cup Olive oil
* 3 1/2 cups Flour
* 2 teaspoons salt
* 1-pound New potatoes; daintily cut, whitened
* 1 cup Julienned red onions
* 2 tablespoons Extra-virgin olive oil
* Salt; to taste
* Freshly-ground white pepper; to taste
* 1/2 cup Grated Parmigiano-Reggiano cheddar
* 1 Drizzle truffle oil
* 2 tablespoons chopped chives

Method:

Preheat the stove 400 degrees. In an electric blender, whisk the yeast, water, and oil, together to frame a glue. Utilizing a battered snare, add the flour and salt to the glue, blend the mixture until the mixture leaves from the sides, and creeps up the sides of the snare. Expel the mixture from the bowl and transform the batter into a lobed bowl, spread. Let the batter ascend until twofold in size, around 60 minutes. Turn the mixture out onto a floured surface and gap into four 4-ounce balls, spread. Let the batter rest for 10 to 15 minutes. Press every batter out into a 10-

INCH hover around 1/2-to 1-INCH thick.

Softly brush the butter with olive oil. Partition the potatoes into four segments and season with salt and pepper. Spread every mixture with the potatoes, leaving a 1-INCH outskirt. In a little blending bowl, hurl the red onions with the extra-virgin olive oil. Season with salt and pepper. Spot a layer of the red onions on the potatoes. Sprinkle every pizza with the ground cheddar. Blend sauce ingredients put in a safe spot. Warmth Oven to 425 degrees Separation batter into equal parts. On gently lobed 12" pizza dish sprinkled with a light covering of corn supper, pat every 50% of batter out into a 10 to 12-inch hover on pizza container. Separation sauce equally between pizza outside layers and spread out. Sprinkle every pizza with 1/4 cup Parmesan Cheese.

Sauté' frankfurter until nearly done, blending to separate. Include the peppers, onions, mushrooms, olives, and pepperoni and keep cooking until frankfurter is done. Dump the skillet brimming with cooked garnishes in a colander to deplete. Channel well overall. Sprinkle fixings equally onto the highest points of pizzas. Sprinkle 1 cup Mozzarella Cheese on every one of the pizzas. Prepare 20 to 25 minutes on the lower rack of the stove at 425 degrees until the hull is dark-colored and filling is hot and bubbly.

Shower every pizza with the truffle oil. Heat for 15 to 20 minutes or until the covering is firm and brilliant dark-colored. Embellishment the pizza with chives.

TURKEY CLUB PIZZA RECIPE:

Ingredients:

* 1 bundle Refrigerated Pizza Dough
* 2 teaspoons sesame seeds
* 1/4 cup Mayonnaise
* 1 teaspoon Lemon pizzazz
* 1 cup Shredded Jack cheddar
* 1/2 tablespoon Basil
* 4 ounces Deli Sliced Turkey Meat
* 6 cuts Bacon - Cooked and Drained
* 1 little Tomato - Thinly Sliced
* 1/2 cup Swiss Cheese - Shredded

Method:

Unroll outside the pizza layer on the pizza or treat sheet. Sprinkle with sesame seeds. Prepare for 10 minutes at 425F degrees. Blend mayo and lemon pizzazz. Spread over covering. Top with unusual ingredients all together recorded and prepared 425F degrees for 7-9 minutes. Warmth stove to 425 degrees. In a little bowl, consolidate mayonnaise, lemon pizzazz, and mustard; mix well. Spread over arranged covering. Cook turkey bacon in a microwave for 4 - 6 minutes. Top pizza with Monterey Jack cheddar, basil, cooked turkey bacon, turkey store cuts, and tomatoes. Sprinkle with Swiss cheddar. Prepare at 425 degrees for 7-9 minutes or until the outside is brilliant darker, and cheddar is liquefied. Spread mayonnaise and mustard equally over the base. Spot 1/2 of the cheddar on mayonnaise base; top with turkey, bacon, and onion. Sprinkle remaining cheddar on top.

Prepare at 425° F for 8 - 10 minutes or until the cheddar is somewhat darker and bubbly. Expel from broiler; top with crisp lettuce and tomatoes. Sprinkle with pepper.

TOPSY TURVY PIZZA RECIPE

Ingredients:

* 1 diced pepper
* 1 diced onion
* Quartered pepperoni cuts
* Diced tomatoes
* Sliced mushrooms
* Shredded mozzarella or provolone
* Italian herbs
* Parmesan cheddar for decorate
* 8-inch rounds of pita bread left entire

Directions:

Preheat a little skillet or omelet dish. Include pepperoni, veggies, and seasonings. Mix for a moment until fresh/delicate and afterward include cheddar. Spot pita on the sautéed blend and press immovably. Cautiously modify a level plate over the dish. Holding container and plate solidly together, flip pizza onto a plate. Top with ground parmesan. Cut into wedges and serve. Dark-colored hamburger, onions, and peppers and blended in different ingredients. Line 9X13 dish with pepperoni cuts. Pour blend on top. Sprinkle on cheddar. For Topping: Mix and pour on meat, sauce, and cheddar blend and prepare for 20 minutes. Other pizza ingredients might be added to the above blend.

WHITE ONION PIZZA RECIPE:

Ingredients:

* 1 formula pizza batter

* 3 medium onions

* 1/4 cup ground Romano cheddar

* 1/2 cup ground/ other white cheddar, for example, mozzarella, white cheddar and so on

* 2 tablespoons additional virgin olive oil

* 3 tablespoons slashed parsley

* anchovies-discretionary

* salt, pepper, garlic powder, dried: oregano, basil, thyme to taste

Method:

No tomato sauce for this pizza, subsequently "'white" pizza. Excellent quality olive oil just as cheeses are significant for best flavor and quality Strip entire onions and bubble 5 minutes and channel. At the point when fresh, cut meager and flush submerged and channel once more. Turn out mixture and spot on pizza dish or warm broiler stone. Sprinkle with olive oil and spread over onions. Sprinkle on cheeses and season to taste with salt, pepper, and herbs. Prepare in a preheated 450 broiler around 20 to 25 minutes. Sprinkle on parsley. Cool 5 minutes before cutting. Cut into 6 to 8 pieces or as wanted. Present with a green serving of mixed greens, and a glass of wine for supper!

Turn covering out to 12" circle. Brush covering with olive oil, sprinkle with garlic and basil. Mastermind tomato cuts over covering and top with ground mozzarella, provolone, and Romano cheeses. Prepare in a hot preheated grill (425 to 450 degrees) 12 to 15 minutes or until cheddar has dissolved, and the outside layer is gently sautéed. Sprinkle with oregano. For best outcomes, heat on material paper straightforwardly on a pizza stone or stone tiles

Mesh the smoked mozzarella; if utilizing new herbs, slash enough thyme and oregano to quantify one teaspoon each. Hack the two garlic cloves. In a little bowl, mix the 1/2 cup ricotta and 1/4 cup mascarpone well and season with salt and a lot of ground dark pepper. Spot the pizza shell on a large preparing dish and brush it with the one tablespoon olive oil; with a spatula, spread the ricotta blend uniformly over the shell. Sprinkle the ground smoked mozzarella over the top, at that point dissipate the one teaspoon every one of new herbs and the two hacked garlic cloves over the mozzarella. Prepare the pizza for 15 minutes or until hot and bubbly. Expel the pizza from the stove and let it rest a moment or two preceding cutting into wedges.

WHITE SPINACH PIZZA RECIPE:

Ingredients:

* 1 (10-OZ) can refrigerated pizza covering
* 1 cup skim milk
* 3 tablespoons universally handy flour
* Salt and pepper to taste
* 1/2-pound mushrooms, cut
* 1/2 teaspoon minced garlic
* 3 cups crisp spinach, washed and stemmed
* 1/2 teaspoon dried basil
* 1/4 cup disintegrated feta
* 1/2 cup part-skim mozzarella cheddar

Method:

Preheat grill to 425°F. Pat outside into a cycle 12-INCH pizza dish covered with nonstock cooking splash. Heat for 7 minutes or until the hull starts to dark-colored. In a little pot, combine milk and flour over medium-high warmth until thickened. Season with salt and pepper to taste. Spread white sauce over the halfway prepared hull. In the meantime, in a skillet covered with a nonstock cooking splash, sauté mushrooms and garlic until delicate, around 5 minutes. Include spinach, mixing until shriveled. Include basil.

Spread spinach blend over the white sauce. Sprinkle with feta and mozzarella cheeses. Come back to the appliance and keep preparing for 10 minutes until the hull is brilliant, dark-colored, and cheddar is softened. Unroll batter and separation into triangles. Roll or press sickle rolls together on a round or square shape pizza skillet or treat sheet. Prepare at 350 degrees for 12-15 minutes or until brilliant dark-colored. Cool totally. Blend cream cheddar, garlic, and one tablespoon of Parmesan cheddar. Spread uniformly over the hull. Top with tomato cuts, cleaved green pepper, green onions, and salami wedges.

ONION PIZZA RECIPE:

Ingredients:

For handcrafted mixture use

* 500 grams rye flour
* 1 teaspoon Salt,
* 1.05 cup tepid water
* 1/4 new yeast (onion pizza) beating:
* 7.14 ounces bacon
* 1000 grams onions
* 2 tablespoons sharp cream
* 2 eggs, Salt,
* 1000 grams onions
* 200 grams bacon
* 4 tablespoons oil,
* Salt and pepper

Method:

For Bread mixture: use locally acquired or make a plain batter (500g to 750g locally acquired bread batter for heating sheet) For the natively constructed batter:

Blend all ingredients, let rise, and turn out onto a lobed heating sheet. Onto these mixtures put various fixings (onion pizza) besting:

Cut exceptionally thick cuts of bacon into solid shapes. Cut up onions and put them into a substantial pot. Sauté until onions are done. Take from stove and add all other fixings to the cooled blend. The blend shouldn't be too fluid. On the off chance that to runny add breadcrumbs to thicken. Put onion besting uniformly on turned out bread batter. Heat at 260*c (500*F) for around 40 to 50 minutes in the stove or until brilliant dark-colored.

Put oil onto bread batter, at that point cubed bacon, and cut onions equitably. Prepare at 260*C (500*F) brilliant dark-colored.

GRILL CHICKEN PIZZA RECIPE:

Ingredients:

* 1 pizza outside

* 6 ounces boneless skinless chicken bosoms

* 2 teaspoons olive oil

* 1/4 cup grill sauce

* 1/2 medium red onion - daintily cut

* 1/2 green chime pepper - diced

* 1/2 cup Monterey jack cheddar

* 1/4 cup new cilantro leaves

Method:

Get ready, Pizza Crust. Preheat grill to 500°F. Cut chicken into 1/4-INCH-THICK strips. Heat 4 cups water to the point of boiling in a huge pot over high warmth. Mix in chicken; spread and expel from heat. Let stand 3 to 4 minutes or until chicken is not, at this point, pink in focus. Channel; put in a safe spot. Brush oil equitably over the arranged hull. Spread grill sauce over covering leaving 1-INCH outskirt. Organize onions over sauce. Top with chicken, chime peppers, and cheddar. Prepare 10 minutes or until the hull is dim brilliant darker. Sprinkle with cilantro and cut into wedges.

Position rack in the focus of the stove. Spot massive heating sheet on rack and preheat broiler to 450F. For 30 minutes.

Warmth olive oil in an overwhelming medium skillet over medium-high warmth. Season chicken with salt and pepper. Add chicken to skillet and sauté until simply cooked through, around 5 minutes for each side. Move chicken to plate; let rest 5 minutes. Cut chicken across into 1/3-inch-wide cuts. Utilizing an opened spoon, move chicken to a medium bowl. Toss with 1/4 cup grill sauce. A spread portion of cheddar on Boboli. Mastermind chicken cuts on Boboli, dividing equitably. Spoon any remaining grill sauce from the bowl over. Sprinkle red onion over chicken. Sprinkle with staying 1/4 cup grill sauce. Sprinkle remaining cheddar and green onion over. Move pizza to the hot preparing sheet. Prepare until the base of the hull is fresh, and cheddar on top melts around 14 minutes. Let pizza stand for 5 minutes.

Warmth stove to 450ºF. Spread heating sheet with hardcore aluminum foil. Flush chicken. Pat dry. Sprinkle with 1/4 teaspoon salt and pepper. Warmth oil in a large skillet on medium-high warmth. Include chicken. Sauté 2 minutes, or until the outside is not, at this point, pink. Expel chicken from the dish with an opened spoon. Add onion and mushrooms to skillet. Sprinkle with staying 1/4 teaspoon salt. Sauté 3 minutes, or until onion is translucent. Expel skillet from heat. Return chicken to the dish. Mix grill sauce into chicken and vegetables. Spot pizza hull on the prepared sheet. Orchestrate half of the cheddar on pizza outside layer. Top with the chicken blend. Top chicken with outstanding cheddar. Heat at 450ºF for 10 to 12 minutes, or until the covering is fresh and cheddar liquefies. Let stand 3 minutes before cutting. Serve right away.

TOP equally with chicken bosom cuts, cheddar, bacon, onion, tomato, and peppers. Spot on the treated sheet. Prepare at 450°F for 8 to 10 minutes or until thoroughly warmed.

PROFOUND DISH MEXICAN PIZZA RECIPE:

Ingredients:

* 1 thick pizza outside layer
* nonstock cooking shower
* 1/2 little onion
* 1 teaspoon bean stew powder
* 1/2 teaspoon ground cumin
* 1/4 teaspoon ground cinnamon
* 15 ounces dark beans - flushed and depleted
* 2 ounces diced green chilies
* cornmeal
* 1 cup Monterey jack cheddar
* 3/4 cup diced tomatoes
* 1/2 cup solidified entire part corn - defrosted
* 1/2 green ringer pepper
* 2 ounces cut ready dark olives - depleted
* 1/2 teaspoon olive oil
* salsa - discretionary

* sour cream - discretionary

Method:

Plan Pizza Crust. Preheat grill to 500°F. Splash 2-to 3-quart pan with cooking shower. Spot over medium warmth. Include onion, stew powder, cumin, cinnamon, and one tablespoon water; mix. Spread and cook 3 to 4 minutes or until onion is fresh delicate. Mix in beans and chilies. Move 1/2 of the bean blend to nourishment processor or blender; process until practically smooth. Splash 14-INCH deep-dish pizza container with nonstock cooking shower; sprinkle with cornmeal. Press mixture delicately into the base and up the side of skillet. Spread with saran wrap and let remain in warm spot 15 to 20 minutes or until puffy. Prepare 5 to 7 minutes or until dry and firm on top. Spread pureed bean blend over outside layer up to the thick edge. Top with a large portion of the cheddar, remaining bean blend, tomatoes, corn, chime pepper, and olives. Top with extra cheddar. Prepare 10 to 12 minutes more or until the covering is profound brilliant. Brush outside layer edges with olive oil. Cut into wedges. Present with salsa and sharp cream.

MAYONNAISE BURRITO PIZZAS RECIPE:

Ingredients:

* 4 flour tortillas

* 8 ounces catsup

* 8 ounces naturally crushed Mayonnaise

* 8 ounces EZ-Cheese American

* 8 ounces EZ-Cheese cheddar

Method:

Preheat grill to 350. Organize the tortillas on the treated sheet. Blend cats up and Mayonnaise in a bowl, separate into four segments, spread each bit onto every tortilla. Top with cheddar, half American and half cheddar. Cook 15-20 minutes. Blend sauce ingredients put in a safe spot. Warmth Oven to 425 degrees Separation batter into equal parts. On gently lobed 12" pizza dish sprinkled with a light covering of corn supper, pat every 50% of batter out into a 10 to 12-inch hover on pizza container. Separation sauce equally between pizza outside layers and spread out. Sprinkle every pizza with 1/4 cup Parmesan Cheese.

Sauté' frankfurter until nearly done, blending to separate. Include the peppers, onions, mushrooms, olives, and pepperoni and keep cooking until frankfurter is done. Dump the skillet brimming with cooked garnishes in a colander to deplete. Channel well overall. Sprinkle fixings equally onto the highest points of pizzas. Sprinkle 1 cup Mozzarella Cheese on every one of the pizzas. Prepare 20 to 25 minutes on the lower rack of the stove at 425 degrees until the hull is dark-colored and filling is hot and bubbly.

Combine the biscuit blend in with the eggs, softened spread, milk, and solidified corn bits. Gently oil a large stove safe non-stick skillet with oil and pour in the biscuit blend. Spot dish in stove and heat 12 to 15 minutes in the focal point of the grill until light brilliant in shading. In another skillet over medium-high warmth, darker the meat, include onions and flavors and cook meat 5 minutes more. Expel cornbread from grill and top with meat, cheddar, and veggies. Add dish back to the grill and cook 5 minutes more to liquefy cheddar. Topping with cilantro, discretionary. Cut into eight wedges and serve the profound dish container pizza from the skillet. Pass taco sauce at the table to sprinkle on top.

Spot pita bread on an enormous heating sheet. In a medium bowl, consolidate beans and Pico de Gallo. Spoon over pita bread. Sprinkle each with cheeses. Prepare 14 to 18 minutes or until warmed through, and cheddar is dissolved. Top with lettuce. Cut each into six wedges. Present with salsa, sharp cream, guacamole, scallions, as well as olives.

Make the batter: In a little pan, heat 1/2 cup water to 110°F. what's more, move to an enormous bowl. Mix in yeast and sugar and let stand 5 minutes, or until frothy. Mix in residual water and batter ingredients to frame a mixture and on a gently floured surface manipulate until smooth and versatile, around 10 minutes. Put batter in a daintily oiled deep bowl, going to cover, and let rise, secured freely, in a warm spot until multiplied in mass, around 60 minutes. (Then again, let batter rise, secured freely, in cooler short-term, or until multiplied in mass.)

Make the sauce: In a 4-quart pan of bubbling water whiten tomatillos one moment and channel in a colander. Cut every tomatillo into eight wedges. In a large, overwhelming skillet cook onion and garlic in oil over moderate warmth, blending sporadically, until onion is pale brilliant. Include tomatillos and cook over moderate warmth, mixing every so often, until tomatillos are mellowed, and the blend is diminished to around 1/4 cups. Fresh blend somewhat and in a nourishment processor purée until smooth. Move sauce to a bowl and mix in coriander, lime squeeze, and salt to taste.

In an enormous substantial skillet cook hotdog over respectably high warmth, mixing and separating bumps until cooked through and seared. Move frankfurter with an opened spoon to paper towels to deplete. Preheat grill to 525°F. furthermore, modify the stove rack on the top rack. Sprinkle a 16-INCH punctured pizza skillet with additional cornmeal. Punch down batter and on a softly floured work surface with a floured folding pin turn out into a 17-INCH circle. Fit batter into skillet, framing an edge, and heat then serve.

A spot outside layer on a massive heating sheet.

In a bowl, join beans and salsa; spread on the hull. Sprinkle on extra fixing except for the cilantro. Heat at 450 degrees F for 10 minutes. Top with cilantro. In a skillet, dark-colored the Lean Ground Beef. Channel off the abundance oil and afterward include the Chili Powder and Cumin. Spread 1/4 cup of the Salsa on each Flour Tortillas and 1/4 of the cooked meat blend. Top with the Shredded Cheddar Cheese and your preferred fixings. Prepare in a pre-warmed 400-degree stove for 8 to 10 minutes.

FLAME-BROILED CHICKEN PIZZA RECIPE

Ingredients:

*   2 boneless, skinless chicken chest parts, cut humble
*   1/2 teaspoon salt, isolated
*   1/4 teaspoon recently ground dull pepper
*   3 tablespoons cooking oil
*   1 medium red onion, stripped and gently cut
*   1 cup gently cut mushrooms
*   1/2 cup hickory-prepared barbecue sauce
*   1 (12-INCH) pre-arranged pizza structure
*   2 cups ground smoked Gouda or devastated mozzarella cheddar

Method:

Warmth stove to 450ºF. Spread a planning sheet with considerable aluminum foil. Wash chicken. Pat dry. Sprinkle with 1/4 teaspoon salt and pepper. Warmth oil in a large skillet on medium-high warmth. Incorporate chicken. Sauté 2 minutes, or until outside isn't, now pink. Remove chicken from skillet with an opened spoon. Add onion and mushrooms to the dish. Sprinkle with remaining 1/4 teaspoon salt.

Sauté 3 minutes, or until onion is translucent. Remove dish from heat. Return chicken to the dish. Blend barbecue sauce into chicken and vegetables. Spot pizza covering on getting ready sheet. Brains half of cheddar on pizza covering. Top with chicken mixture. Top chicken with lingering cheddar. Get ready at 450ºF for 10 to 12 minutes, or until the body is new and cheddar breaks up. Let stand 3 minutes before cutting. Serve immediately.

BARBECUE CHICKEN AND BACON PIZZA RECIPE:

Ingredients:

* 2 Italian pizza structures (6 to 7 inch)

* 1/4 cup Barbecue Sauce

* 1 group (6 oz. size) Oven Roasted Chicken Breast Meat

* 3/4 cup Shredded Cheddar or Mozzarella Cheese

* 1/2 cup Cooked and Chopped Bacon Pieces

* 1/4 cup each hacked green onion, tomato, and ring pepper

Method:

SPREAD pizza frames with flame broil sauce. TOP similarly with chicken chest cuts, cheddar, bacon, onion, tomato, and peppers. Spot on the treated sheet. Get ready at 450°F for 8 to 10 minutes or until through and through warmed. Preheat grill to 425 degrees F (220 degrees C). In a pot over medium-high warmth, solidify chicken, barbecue sauce, nectar, molasses, darker sugar, and cilantro. Warmth to the point of bubbling. Spread chicken mix consistently over pizza frame and top with cheddar and onions. Get ready for 15 to 20 minutes or until the cheddar is relaxed.

Spot covering on a getting ready sheet. Get ready at 450 degrees for 3 minutes. Remove from oven; spread chutney over outside layer, leaving a 1/2-INCH periphery. Top chutney with chicken. Sprinkle diced tomato, cheddar, and green onions consistently over chicken. Get ready at 450 degrees for 9 minutes or until cheddar breaks up. Cut pizza into wedges.

BOURSIN CHICKEN PIZZA RECIPE:

Ingredients:

* 1 pizza covering
* 1/4 cup dry white wine
* 1 tablespoon lemon juice
* 2 tablespoons olive oil
* 1 clove garlic
* 1/2 teaspoon dried oregano leaves
* 1/2 teaspoon dried basil leaves
* 1/2 teaspoon dim pepper
* 1-pound boneless skinless chicken chest
* nonstock cooking shower
* 3/4 cup crumbled light bourse cheddar
* 1/2 cup cut fresh basil
* 2 tablespoons cut fresh chives

Method:

Plan Pizza Crust. Join white wine, lemon juice, one tablespoon olive oil, garlic, oregano, basil, and pepper in a medium bowl. Move wine mix to great resealable plastic sustenance storing sack. Add chicken to pack; seal sack and employ to cover chicken with marinade. Spot in cooler and marinate at any rate 2 hours or overnight. Oust chicken from marinade; discard exceptional marinade. Sprinkle large nonstick skillet with cooking shower; heat over medium warmth until hot. Incorporate chicken; cook and blend 12 to 15 minutes or until chicken is splendid dim shaded and not, now pink in center. Bright chicken to cutting board. Exactly when chicken is adequately cool to manage, cut into 1/2-INch pieces.

Preheat oven to 450°F. Brush blend with remaining one tablespoon olive oil. Top with chicken, Boursin cheddar, basil, and chives. Get ready 18 to 20 minutes or until the outside layer is splendid dim shaded, and cheddar is mollified.

WILD BULL CHICKEN WING PIZZA RECIPE:

Ingredients:

* 3/4-pound chicken pieces
* 1/2 cup flour
* 1/2 cup oil, to fry the chicken
* 1/2 cup chicken wing sauce, moment
* 3 ounces hot sauce
* 6 tablespoons margarine - condensed
* 1/4 cup blue cheddar dressing
* 4 ounces mozzarella cheddar
* 3 tablespoons blue cheddar
* 1 medium pizza outside layer

Method:

Mix flour and Cajun seasoning (I use Emeril's Essence) in a plastic pack. Put chicken pieces dealt with (1 or 2 on the double) and shake until secured with flour mix. Warmth oil in a fry holder. Incorporate chicken and cook, turning from time to time, for around 20 minutes.

Preheat oven to 425 degrees F. Empty chicken and grant to adequately cool to manage. Cut chicken into pieces around 1/2" in width. Shake around two teaspoons of hot sauce onto the chicken (or to taste). Spread pizza hitter onto a lobed dish, around 14" width. Mix chicken wing sauce with blue cheddar dressing. Spread the sauce mix onto the pizza player. Spread the bits of chicken onto the top of the sauce. Sprinkle wrecked mozzarella over the chicken. Sprinkle the crumbled blue cheddar on top of the mozzarella. Warmth at 425 F for around 20 minutes, or until cheddar is gently sung.

In a little bowl, separate the nectar in the warm water. Sprinkle the yeast over the water and blend until it separates. Let the yeast mix speak to 5 minutes, until a layer of foam outlines on a superficial level. In a large bowl, merge the flour and the salt. Make a well in the point of convergence of the flour mix and pour the olive oil and the yeast mix. Blend the flour into the wet ingredients until all the flour is joined. In case it's exorbitantly dry, incorporate more water. On a gently floured surface, handle the player for 15 minutes, until it is smooth and adaptable. Shape the hitter into a ball and put it in an inside and out of the oiled bowl. Spread with a wet towel and let climb in a warm spot until twofold in mass (around 1/2 hours). One hour before setting up the pizzas, start preheating the stove with pizza stones inside at 500 degrees F.

For the Chicken

In a large skillet, heat the olive oil on medium-high warmth. Incorporate chicken pieces. sauté until cooked (6 minutes). Chill. Coat chicken with two tablespoons flame broil sauce. Set aside in the cooler.

Punch the player down, and parcel into four equal fragments. Uncover each piece into a 6-8-inch level circle. Spread 1/4 cup flame broil sauce over the outside of the blend. Scatter 1/2 of the cheddar over the sauce. Proper 1/2 of the chicken over the cheddar. Spot half of the onion rings over the chicken pieces. Recognize the pizza in the stove (on pizza stones). Warmth until the structure is firm, and cheddar is frothing (8-10 minutes). Remove pizzas from the stove and sprinkle each with 1/2 of the cilantro.

CALIFORNIA PIZZA KITCHEN'S THAI CHICKEN PIZZA RECIPE:

Ingredients:

* 1 cup warm water
* 2 teaspoons dry yeast
* 3 cups flour
* 1 teaspoon salt Topping
* 3 1/2 tablespoons nutty spread
* 3 tablespoons tea
* 3 tablespoons rice vinegar
* 2 tablespoons soy sauce
* 2 teaspoons bean stew oil
* 1 tablespoon ginger, minced
* 1/2 teaspoon sesame oil
* 2 tablespoons sesame seeds, toasted
* 1 1/2 tablespoon green onions
* 1/2-pound chicken chest, cut in 1/4-INCH strips
* 1/2 cup mozzarella cheddar, crushed
* 1 carrot, crushed

* 1/4 cup cilantro, sliced

Method:

For the blend: In a little bowl, separate the nectar in the warm water. Sprinkle the yeast over the water and blend until it separates. Let the yeast mix speak to 5 minutes, until a layer of foam outlines on a superficial level.

In a large bowl, merge the flour and the salt. Make a well in the point of convergence of the flour mix and pour the olive oil and the yeast mix. Blend the flour into the wet ingredients until all the flour is joined. If it's too dry, incorporate more water. On a delicately floured surface, knead the hitter for 15 minutes, until it is smooth and adaptable. Shape the player into a ball and put in an especially oiled bowl. Spread with a wet towel and let rise in a warm spot until twofold.

BURRITO MEXICALI PIZZA RECIPE:

Ingredients:

*   1 box single cheddar pizza blend
*   1 (4 oz.) can slash green chilie
*   1 (16 oz.) can refried beans
*   2 tablespoons bean stew flavoring
*   1/4 teaspoon Tabasco
*   8 ounces ground cheddar
*   1/2-pound caramelized ground meat
*   1 onion, slashed
*   1 green pepper, cut in strips
*   1 tomato, slashed

Method:

Plan batter as coordinated on the box; include 2 ounces of green chilies to the mixture. Combine refried beans, stew flavoring, Tabasco, and remaining chilies. Spread equally over mixture. Include sauce, ground cheddar from the box, and ground cheddar. Top with cooked ground meat, cleaved onion, green pepper strips, tomato pieces, and olives. Prepare for 20 minutes at 425 degrees.

Get ready, Pizza Crust. Preheat stove to 500°F. Splash 2-to 3-

quart pan with cooking shower. Spot over medium warmth. Include onion, bean stew powder, cumin, cinnamon, and one tablespoon water; mix. Spread and cook 3 to 4 minutes or until onion is fresh delicate. Mix in beans and chilies. Move 1/2 of the bean blend to nourishment processor or blender; process until practically smooth. Shower 14-INCH deep-dish pizza container with a nonstock cooking splash; sprinkle with cornmeal. Press batter tenderly into the base and up the side of skillet. Spread with saran wrap and let remain in warm spot 15 to 20 minutes or until puffy. Heat 5 to 7 minutes or until dry and firm on top. Spread pureed bean blend over covering up to the thick edge. Top with a large portion of the cheddar, remaining bean blend, tomatoes, corn, chime pepper, and olives. Top with outstanding cheddar. Prepare 10 to 12 minutes more or until the hull is profound brilliant. Brush covering edges with olive oil. Cut into wedges. Present with salsa and sharp cream.

COLORADO CALZONI:

Ingredients:

1) 1 recipe for pizza dough,
2) 1 refrigerated pizza dough
3) 1/2 c. yellow squash, chopped
4) 1/2 c. zucchini, chopped
5) 1/2 c. bell pepper, chopped
6) 1/2 c. eggplant, chopped
7) 1/2 c. onion, chopped
8) 1/2 c. favorite pesto
9) 1 c. favorite cheese, shredded
10) olive oil, salt and peppersharp cream.

Method:

In a colossal sauté skillet, cook the vegetables (squash through onion) in a little olive oil over medium warmth, until mellowed and starting to brown. Remove from the gleam and put in a protected spot.

Preheat the stove to 425°. On a floured surface, reveal the pizza mix into a 16" circle. On half of the circle, spread half of the pesto and cheddar, leaving in any event a one inch at the edge of the mix. Spread the sautéed vegetables reliably over the pesto and cheddar, and top with the rest of the pesto and cheddar. Wrinkle the mix over and smash the sides passionately to seal.

Make two or three little cuts in the most raised reason for the calzone to permit the steam to get away. Warmth on a preparing sheet for around 20-30 minutes, until the outside layer is starting to brown. Cut into fourths and serve right away.

Leave a review of my book. For us authors, they are essential for improving and writing other useful content for readers! If you liked...

"BREAD AND PIZZA BAKING" leaves five stars!

Leave your review from this link:

https://www.amazon.com/review/create-review/error?ie=UTF8&channel=glance-detail&asin=B087NBL8SD

Thanks for the support is highly appreciated!

THE END

www.ingramcontent.com/pod-product-compliance
Lightning Source LLC
Chambersburg PA
CBHW052354220526
45465CB00003BA/1097